T0383506

THE LITTLE BOOK OF

STOIC
WISDOM

Also by Joseph Piercy

Life Lessons from Literature

THE LITTLE BOOK OF

STOIC WISDOM

LEARN THE ART OF LIVING WELL WITH CLASSICAL PHILOSOPHY

JOSEPH PIERCY

Michael O'Mara Books Limited

First published in Great Britain in 2025 by

Michael O'Mara Books Limited
9 Lion Yard
Tremadoc Road
London SW4 7NQ

A CIP catalogue record for this book is available from the British Library.

This product is made of material from well-managed, FSC®-certified forests and other controlled sources. The manufacturing processes conform to the environmental regulations of the country of origin.

ISBN: 978-1-78929-728-7 in hardback print format
ISBN: 978-1-78929-782-9 in trade paperback print format
ISBN: 978-1-78929-729-4 in ebook format

1 2 3 4 5 6 7 8 9 10

Cover design by Barbara Ward, using an illustration from Shutterstock
Designed and typeset by Claire Cater

Printed and bound by CPI Group (UK) Ltd, Croydon, CR0 4YY

www.mombooks.com

For further information see www.mombooks.com/about/sustainability-climate-focus

Report any safety issues to product.safety@mombooks.com

Contents

For Polly

Introduction

Why Stoicism?

What can escort us on our way? One thing, and one thing only: philosophy. This consists in keeping the divinity within us inviolate and free from harm, master of pleasure and pain, doing nothing without aim, truth, or integrity and independent of other's actions or failure to act.[1]

Meditations – Marcus Aurelius, Book II

1   Marcus Aurelius, *Meditations*, trans. Hammond, Martin, Penguin Random House, London, 2006, p15

The *Oxford English Dictionary* defines the word 'stoic' as 'a person who is able to suffer pain or trouble without complaining or showing what they are feeling'.[2] This has remained more or less how the word has been understood since its first appearance in the English language around the fifteenth century. We often hear people who have suffered a misfortune or setback described as being 'stoical' because they seem to be coping well, or don't seem to be as distressed as we imagine they would be. This has led to a misconception of Stoicism as a school of thought, that it promotes the suppression of emotions and natural desires; that Stoics are repressed lumps of granite unable to express human feelings. However, while it is true that one aspect of Stoicism concerns resilience in the face of adversity, Stoicism is much more than just 'taking it on the chin' and 'moving on'.

Stoicism is a philosophy that originated in ancient Greece and was first developed by Zeno of Citium around 300 BC. He taught at a painted colonnade or porch (*stoa*) in the centre of Athens, from which the philosophy's name is derived. It was in Rome however, some two centuries later, that Stoic principles and ideas came to fruition and were promoted by the senator and playwright Seneca; by Epictetus, who was

---

2 https://www.oxfordlearnersdictionaries.com/definition/english/stoic_1

an ex-slave turned philosopher; and by the Emperor Marcus Aurelius. Initially Stoicism comprised various disciplines, including formal logic, grammar, physics, meteorology and rhetoric, but it was in its development of an ethical code suggesting how to live a good life that Stoicism as a philosophy found its voice.

It might seem odd to take the thoughts of three very different philosophers from ancient Rome and apply them to modern society. You might think that the day-to-day issues which concerned Epictetus, who was born in slavery, were vastly different from the daily concerns of you or I. Although were they? Perhaps we need to step back and look at this from a wider perspective – 'take the view from above', as the Stoics say. Has the rudimentary question of how to live really changed in the last two thousand years? People are still unhappy, frustrated, fearful, hurt, angry, depressed and riddled with anxieties – maybe more so than ever. So can an ancient philosophy address these basic issues that afflict all of us from time to time?

Firstly, Stoicism is a practical philosophy which values actions and deeds over theoretical contemplation (although thinking things through before acting is, paradoxically, part of the process). It is a 'can do' philosophy rather than a 'why can I do?' approach to life.

At its core is the belief that it isn't things themselves – whether people, situations or circumstances – that cause us distress, it's how we view them: our judgements. In this sense it is all in the mind, and if we can train ourselves to make better judgements we can eliminate the pain, hurt and anxieties that beleaguer us. Stoicism seeks to control negative notions such as fear, anger or jealousy, not only because they are based on flawed judgements, but also because they do not help one to live a stress-free life, and they often lead to bad outcomes and strife.

The Stoics also believed it was wrong to put faith in circumstances or things that are commonly considered good in themselves or as necessary prerequisites to living a happy life. These could be money, good health, social status or material possessions. These things Stoics label as 'externals'. While most people would like to live in a nice house and not have to worry about paying the bills, these external things do not in themselves guarantee happiness, contentment and a joyful life.

All that we have control over is our thoughts and our character, and to have a mind that functions according to reason and a virtuous character are all that are needed to live a good life, to live, as the Stoics say, as the 'best version of ourselves'. The Stoics believe that it is possible to live well in any circumstances if we adopt the correct mindset. External circumstances can and will present us with obstacles and setbacks (some Stoics relish the challenge, as we shall see), but as long as we adopt the right frame of mind we can be resolute and resilient when buffeted by the cruel and fickle winds of misfortune.

Epictetus writes that you should 'settle on the type of person you want to be and stick to it, whether alone or in company'.[3] We all aspire to be good people, and therefore our 'attention' needs to be on cultivating the right state of mind. Stoics use the term 'attention' in a specific way, not as in paying attention in class, but instead as paying attention to the judgements we make and avoiding negative and damaging emotions. It is an old-fashioned meaning of the verb 'to attend to', as in 'to look after and watch over'. Like gardeners attending to plants, we must attend to our character and nurture positive traits such as the virtues of courage, justice, moderation and wisdom, which will allow us to grow as human beings. This nature metaphor is particularly apposite, as the goal for the Stoics is to live in accordance with Nature. This is reflected in some core Stoic values such as being consistent in our beliefs and values, and maintaining harmony with our place in the natural order as a whole.

---

3 Epictetus, *Discourses and Selected Writings*, trans. and ed. Dobbin, Robert, Penguin Random House, London, 2008, p236

To be Stoic requires developing a skill set, a toolkit of mental processes that takes practice and is a process, not an end product. It is a lifelong project and not something that someone can try for a while to see if it suits them. There will be bumps along the way, but mistakes are all part of the learning process. The object is for these mistakes and errors of judgement to become fewer and fewer so that life can flow smoothly like the currents of a river running out into a tranquil, sunlit sea (Marcus Aurelius was always fond of a river metaphor).

This book is just a starting point which I hope will encourage people to take up Stoicism as a guide to mindfulness and living well. I have covered the key areas and concepts of the philosophy and provide some practical examples of how it can apply to our everyday lives. Many people are turning to Stoicism and finding comfort in its values and simple, straightforward, no-nonsense approach to the obstacles and issues of modern life. I hope this book encourages more people to take on the Stoic project. It is easy to become despondent in the face of all the violence and divisions, hatred and vitriol that confront us on a seemingly daily basis, so if a few more people commit to cultivating the virtues of compassion, tolerance, moderation and courage embodied by Stoicism, the world would be one that we all want to live in. Good luck and look after yourselves and others.

A NOTE ON TRANSLATIONS AND CITATIONS

One of the issues with using quotations from the writings of Seneca, Epictetus and Marcus Aurelius is that there are lots of different translations, which often differ quite noticeably in terms of expression. The core message is more or less the same but the emphasis of certain words sometimes renders meaning more ambiguous or open to interpretation. I have taken as my main source for all three writers the Penguin Classic editions but got a little derailed by Seneca's letters, largely because the editor and translator of the Penguin edition, Robin Campbell, omitted some letters that he felt were repetitive or dull or just Seneca going off on a tangent about non-Stoic-related verbal ephemera. So for those additional letters, I used an online version of some of Seneca's works via Wikisource, which I found to be an excellent resource. In terms of the citations, I have used Roman numerals for Marcus Aurelius and Seneca's as this is how they are most commonly presented, whereas Epictetus is cited by standard numbering for chapters in the *Enchiridion* and Roman numerals in the *Discourses*, just to confuse matters.

Joseph Piercy

PART ONE

THE WISDOM OF THE ANCIENTS

A brief history of the life and work of the principal Stoic philosophers

Chapter One

Life Under the Painted Porch

He that is perfectly wise is perfectly happy;
nay, the very beginning of wisdom makes life
easy to us. It is not enough to know this; we
must print it in our minds by daily meditation,
and so bring a good will to a good habit.[4]

'On a Happy Life' (*De Vita Beata*) –
Seneca the Younger

---

4   Seneca, *Dialogues and Essays*, trans. Davie, John, Oxford University
Press, Oxford, 2008, pp85–112

At the northern edge of the Ancient Agora of Athens stood the *Stoa Poikile*, the 'Painted Portico' or 'Painted Porch'. *Stoas* in ancient Greece were covered walkways or colonnades and were part of a public meeting place called an *agora*. Politicians would come to the *stoa* to make announcements and proclamations; legal trials and arbitrations took place under the *stoa*; ceremonies and sacrifices to the gods were enacted; tradesmen set up stalls to advertise and sell their wares and, perhaps most importantly, philosophers gathered there to talk and teach anyone who would listen.

The Cynic philosopher Crates of Thebes (365–285 BC), who famously gave away his wealth to live on the streets with the poor of Athens, is thought to have squatted in the *stoa*, as it was there he learnt from the philosopher Diogenes (404–323 BC). Crates was known as the 'door opener' on account of his popularity, as it was said that he could knock on the door of any dwelling in Athens and he would be warmly welcomed inside. The Greek historian

Plutarch (AD 46–119) describes Crates as displaying an indomitably cheerful disposition and living every day 'as if he were at a festival'. Much revered for his wisdom and calmness of mind, Crates was often called upon to arbitrate arguments and disputes and to bring about reconciliations with his 'soothing rhetoric' and 'gentle judgement'. Perhaps Crates' greatest contribution to history, however, was as the teacher of Zeno of Citium (334–262 BC), the founder of the Stoic school of philosophy.

US President Theodore Roosevelt took a copy of Marcus Aurelius' *Meditations* with him on his perilous expedition down the River of Doubt in 1912. Roosevelt and his son Kermit set out to explore and map an unknown Amazonian tributary, and Roosevelt wrote of the strength and resilience he drew from reading *Meditations*.

Zeno was born in the Phoenician colony of Citium (Larnaca in present-day Cyprus). There is some dispute over his ancestry, as although Citium had been an outpost of the Phoenician empire since the twelfth century BC and had periods of both Egyptian and Persian rule, it had a large Greek population dating back to around 1100 BC, the aftermath of the Trojan War. What is known of Zeno's life is mostly contained in much later historical accounts such as Diogenes Laërtius' *Lives and Opinions of Eminent Philosophers*, which contains a biography of Zeno. According to this, Zeno became interested in philosophy after visiting the Oracle at Delphi to ask about how to achieve personal fulfilment in life. The Oracle told him he should 'adopt the complexions of the dead', which Zeno interpreted to mean he should study the wisdom of the ancients.

A wealthy merchant, Zeno was travelling by ship between Phoenicia (in modern Lebanon) and the Greek port of Piraeus when he was shipwrecked. Zeno lost his entire livelihood in the storm and made his way to Athens where he tried to re-establish his business. After reading about Socrates in Xenophon's *Memorabilia*, a collection of Socratic dialogues, Zeno rushed to a bookseller to enquire where such men as Socrates could be found and the bookseller introduced him to Crates, who happened to be passing by.[5] This

---

5   Diogenes Laërtius, *Lives of Eminent Philosophers*, trans Mensch, Pamela, ed Miller, James, Oxford University Press, Oxford, 2008, p305

moment of serendipity had a profound influence on Zeno's view of fate and adversity, for having survived the trauma of the shipwreck, he had the subsequent good fortune to meet Crates, a man who changed the course of his life. According to Laërtius, Zeno often later remarked, 'I made a prosperous journey when I suffered shipwreck.'[6]

There is an argument that Stoicism had different branches or factions and that it wasn't, in fact, a unified school of thought. The Greek/Egyptian writer Athenaeus, writes in his work *Deipnosophistae* ('dinner table philosophers') that there were three branches of Stoicism following the different teachings of the last three heads of the Stoic school: Diogenes, Antipater, and Panaetius.

---

6   Ibid., p305

Zeno studied under Crates for several years and also took instruction from several other philosophers before starting his own school of philosophy. At first Zeno and his students were known as the Zenonians but later the name changed to the Stoics as all of their meetings and teaching took place in the *Stoa Poikile*. Among Zeno's followers was a young boxer named Cleanthes who became the head of the school on Zeno's death. Cleanthes in turn taught Chrysippus, a precocious young Phoenician who, like Zeno, arrived in Athens on the back of misfortune after having been cheated out of his property and wealth. Chrysippus became Cleanthes' star pupil and the natural successor as the head of the school upon Cleanthes' death.

Worth More Than its Weight in Gold

Zeno was in the business of trading in fabric dyes, in particular murex, which is produced from the mucus of carnivorous sea snails. Murex yields a pigment known as Tyrian Purple which was one of the most prized commodities in antiquity, worth three times its weight in gold. The dye created a shimmering reddish-purple colour that, due to its rarity and the complex process of extracting the dye, was only used on fabrics and garments for the extremely powerful and wealthy. Cleopatra is alleged to have had all the sails on her royal barge dyed Tyrian Purple and it was the symbolic colour of the robes of the High Priests of Jerusalem. Tyrian Purple was the colour of Julius Caesar's toga, and an edict was passed in Rome that only the emperor was permitted to wear the colour. To transgress this law was tantamount to treason and punishable by death. The term 'murex' for the particular species of snail was a taxonomy first coined by the philosopher Aristotle (384–382 BC) in his pioneering work on zoology, *The History of Animals.*

By establishing a line of succession with pupils training to become teachers, the Stoics became the pre-eminent Athenian school of thought for several centuries until the centre of Stoic thought shifted to Rome. In the second century BC the Romans began their conquest of Greece, and imposed a military tax upon Athens. In response, in 155 BC a delegation of philosophers – Diogenes of Babylon, the head of the Stoics, along with two representatives of the Peripatetic school (founded by Aristotle) – were sent to Rome on a diplomatic mission to give a series of public lectures in defence of Athens. The somewhat conventional and conformist Romans were stirred by the progressive ideas and radical rhetoric that Diogenes and others were promoting, and this inspired the development of the Roman branch of Stoicism that flourished for nearly five centuries and produced the influential ideas of Seneca, Epictetus and Marcus Aurelius that serve as the bedrock of Stoic thought today.

Chapter Two

The Rise of
the Romans

The happiness of your life depends upon
the quality of your thoughts: therefore,
guard accordingly, and take care that
you entertain no notions unsuitable
to virtue and reasonable nature.[7]

Meditations – Marcus Aurelius, Book III

---

7   Marcus Aurelius, *Meditations*, p20.

The first of the famous Roman Stoics was Lucius Annaeus Seneca (*c*.4 BC – AD 65), who lived a very eventful life. Seneca was a polymath, widely versed in both Greek and Latin, as well as the arts and sciences, he wrote tragedies, poems, essays, speeches and made a lasting contribution to philosophy at the same time as being a politician, political advisor and successful businessman.

Marcus Aurelius appears as a character in the Oscar-winning film *Gladiator,* played by Richard Harris. In the film Marcus is murdered by his son Commodus: in real life it is thought that Marcus Aurelius died of the Antoine Plague, aged fifty-eight.

Seneca the Younger, as he was commonly known, was born in the Roman colony of Córdoba, Spain – a city renowned as one of the centres of intellectual excellence in the Roman Empire. Seneca however, moved to Rome with his aunt when he was around five years old, and as befitting Roman nobility, was instructed in rhetoric, grammar and philosophy. His teacher was the early Roman Stoic philosopher Attalus. Seneca had a rapacious appetite for knowledge and in one of his letters (which often quote Attalus), he (Seneca) 'laid siege to his [Attalus'] lecture hall, always first to arrive and last to go and would draw him into discussion on some point or other even when he just out taking a walk'.[8]

Seneca was plagued by ill health throughout his life. He probably suffered from chronic asthma and it is thought that at some point he contracted tuberculosis. He moved to Egypt to recuperate, living with his aunt and her husband, who was the Roman governor of Egypt.

In AD 31, the three returned to Rome but the ship sank and Seneca's uncle died. It was the first of many trials and upheavals that would befall Seneca throughout his colourful life and influence his ideas of Stoicism.

---

8   Seneca, *Letters from a Stoic,* trans. Campbell, Robin, Penguin Random House, London, 2004, p201.

Given his family background and upbringing, Seneca was destined to enter politics and became a Roman senator, which he did around AD 37, in the reign of Caligula. Renowned for his oratorical skills, Seneca rapidly became a popular and powerful voice in the senate, a fact which is thought to have enraged the volatile and jealous Caligula who, according to some sources, ordered Seneca to commit suicide (the method of execution for Roman noblemen) on the grounds of treason. Seneca's health had deteriorated again and Caligula's sentence was not upheld as Caligula believed Seneca was probably going to die soon anyway.

Following Caligula's assassination in 41, Claudius became emperor and Seneca was immediately embroiled in another political intrigue. The new empress, Messalina, accused Seneca of adultery and conspiring against Claudius with Caligula's sister, and Seneca was sentenced to death by the senate. Claudius, however, changed the sentence to enforced exile and Seneca was sent to live on Corsica, which he described as a 'barren and thorny rock'.

Marcus Aurelius was fifteen years old when Epictetus died. The Emperor Hadrian adopted Marcus' uncle, who in turn adopted Marcus which put him in line to inherit the throne of Rome. The only direct link between Epictetus is through Hadrian, an avowed *philhellene*, (a lover of the history and culture of Greece) who is thought to have been a personal friend of Epictetus and taken instruction at Epictetus' school in Nicopolis.

Despite his protestations to the contrary, Seneca's time on Corsica was probably relatively comfortable. It is likely that he was allowed to take his family and his slaves with him along with his not inconsiderable fortune. Corsica had been a province of the Roman Empire since the second century BC, providing wood and iron ore, and the Romans had planted vineyards to produce cheap wine for export across the empire.

During his time on the island, Seneca was able,

through the prism of exile, to reflect upon the trials and tribulations of his life by writing essays and poems which he sent to his friends and allies. Of particular significance during this period were the three *Consolations*, letters offering solace at a time of personal grief to his mother; to the daughter of a wealthy Roman teacher and historian; and to a secretary of Emperor Claudius. Although ostensibly letters, the *Consolations* are written in the form of philosophical and rhetorical arguments on the nature of adversity, sorrow and death.

In the letter to his mother 'Consolation to Helvia' (*De Consolatione ad Helviam Matrem*), Seneca gives a clear outline of the Stoic attitude to circumstances that are beyond an individual's control, and offers the philosophy's advice to be prepared for challenges of misfortune and hardship:

'External circumstances have very little importance either for good or for evil: the wise man is neither elated by prosperity nor depressed by adversity; for he has always endeavoured to depend chiefly upon himself and to derive all his joys from himself.'[9]

Seneca reminds his mother that she has endured great suffering in the past and can draw strength from the fortitude and resilience she has acquired from her experiences:

---

9   Seneca, *Consolation to Helvia*, trans. Stewart, Aubrey, The Talking Book, (Kindle Edition), London, 2023

'You have gained nothing by so many misfortunes, if you have not learned how to suffer . . .'[10]

In AD 49, the empress Messalina was murdered and Claudius married his niece Agrippina, who was sympathetic to Seneca and persuaded the emperor to recall him to Rome as a personal tutor to her son Nero.

When Nero became emperor of Rome in AD 54 he was sixteen years old, and so Seneca, as his tutor and confidant, also became his advisor and chief speechwriter. This afforded Seneca considerable influence over the young emperor in the early years of his reign. However, following the murder of Agrippina in AD 59, on Nero's orders, a reluctant Seneca was forced to write a letter to the Roman senate justifying the matricide. From then on his influence over Nero began to fade.

---

10 Ibid.

Was Seneca a Hypocrite?

After his return from exile, Seneca's influence over Nero gave him access to resources and opportunities which allowed for him to amass vast personal wealth. Alongside properties in Rome, Seneca owned several large country villas and estates, including vineyards, in other Roman provinces and parts of the empire such as Egypt. Various Roman historians have suggested that Seneca's wealth was gained through corrupt means and through usurious moneylending schemes. There is even a suggestion by some scholars that Boudica's uprising in AD 60 against the Roman occupation of Britain was provoked in part by Seneca's loans and taxation. Seneca's pursuit of wealth seems at odds with the Stoic view that wealth in itself is not intrinsically valuable, and that focusing on wealth is a distraction from living a life of virtue, which is where true value lies. Seneca tries to justify the acquisition of wealth on philosophical lines in his essay 'On a Happy Life' (*De Vita Beata*), where he argues that what is important is a person's attitude to wealth, and that if he were to lose everything he had he would be grateful for the challenge of adversity and not be any less happy. Nevertheless, it is hard, in the face of multiple accusations of corruption and being an unscrupulous loan shark, not to feel that Seneca perhaps didn't always practise what he preached.

Seneca made several attempts to withdraw from public life and retire to his country estates to write, but the progressively unhinged Nero refused to let him. With his influence over Nero broken and in fear of falling foul of the paranoid emperor's purges of his enemies, real or imagined, Seneca spent the last years of his life writing philosophical works, most notably 'Moral Epistles to Lucilius' (*Epistulae Morales ad Lucilium*), a collection of 124 letters to his friend Lucilius which outline the principles of Seneca's Stoic philosophy and view on life.

In AD 65, several prominent Roman statesmen were involved in a conspiracy to murder Nero and replace him with a senator named Gaius Calpurnius Piso. The plot failed and the principal conspirators were ordered to commit suicide. Although there is little evidence that Seneca was involved, according to the Roman historian Tacitus, there were rumours of another conspiracy that planned to use Piso to kill Nero and then execute him and make Seneca emperor. The rumour was enough for Nero to demand that Seneca should commit suicide, along with an estimated forty other people. Seneca killed himself by the favoured Roman method of opening his veins and bleeding to death in a warm bath.

First tell yourself what you want to be, then act your part accordingly.[11]

Discourses – Epictetus, Book III, Chapter 23

The second of the triumvirate of great Roman Stoics was Epictetus (AD 55–135), whose early life could not have contrasted more with the aristocratic Seneca. Epictetus was born into a slave family in the Hellenistic city of Hierapolis, the remains of which can be found in modern south-western Turkey. The name *epíktētos* in Greek means 'acquired' or 'property' and so was almost certainly the name given to him by his master, Epaphroditus, who was a freedman (former slave) who worked as a secretary and scribe for the Emperor Nero. Some scholars, most notably Tacitus, have suggested that Epaphroditus was responsible

---

11   Epictetus, *Discourses*, p168

for unmasking the Piso conspiracy against Nero, and in reward for his loyalty, Nero promoted him to high military office. This new status and wealth allowed him to free Epictetus from servitude some time around AD 68. There is fitting synchronicity in the idea that the incident that caused Seneca's death simultaneously gave birth to Epictetus' freedom to practise philosophy.

Epictetus developed a passion for philosophy at a young age and as the slave of an imperial secretary he was permitted to be educated. He studied under Musonius Rufus, the foremost Stoic philosopher in Rome at that time. After being granted his freedom, Epictetus formed his own school of philosophy in Rome and developed and taught his brand of Stoicism relatively unhindered until AD 93, when the Emperor Domitian, a stern autocrat, became suspicious of the influence of philosophers and exiled from Rome anybody found teaching the discipline.

Sent into exile, in true Stoical fashion Epictetus turned adversity into opportunity, and moved to the Greek city of Nicopolis on the Adriatic coast, where he set up a new school. It became a great success and attracted students from several countries, most notably the sons of Roman noblemen who wished their children to be educated by Greek methods, which were regarded as sophisticated and exotic. It is thought that the young Emperor Hadrian, who had a great love of

Greek philosophy and literature, may have spent some time at Epictetus' school.

Although after Domitian's assassination the ban on philosophers was lifted, Epictetus never returned to Rome and lived out the rest of his life in quiet seclusion with very little by way of material wealth. Late in life, Epictetus, who never married, adopted an orphan and employed a woman to help nurse and raise the child as his son. Epictetus died in AD 135 at the ripe old age of eighty-five after a long and fruitful life.

US Grammy award-winning R&B artist T-Pain is a follower of Stoicism and paid tribute to the philosophy on his 2015 album *Stoicville*. The album is an autobiographical account of the singer's troubled childhood and struggles with alcohol and depression, and how he overcame those obstacles through Stoic practices.

Epictetus did not write any works himself. Instead, in the manner of Socrates, whose thoughts were recorded by his student Plato, Epictetus' teachings were recorded by his student Arrian. Epictetus' principal work is known as the *Discourses*, of which four books survive (four have been lost), comprising of transcripts of Epictetus' lectures purportedly recorded 'word for word' by Arrian. A second work, titled the *Enchiridion* ('Handbook'), is a digest of Epicetetus' principal themes and ideas.

Epictetus has had an enormous influence on Western philosophy with aspects of his thought providing inspiration for major figures throughout history from Marcus Aurelius (see below) to Blaise Pascal, René Descartes and Michel Foucault.

You are a soul carrying a corpse
as Epictetus used to say.[12]

Meditations – Marcus Aurelius, Book IV

Called the 'Philosopher King', Marcus Aurelius Antoninus (121–180) was born in Rome to a high-ranking

---

12   Ibid., p31

family. His father was a politician and magistrate, and he was related by marriage to the Emperor Hadrian. Marcus' father died when he was an infant and he was unofficially adopted by his paternal grandfather before being formally adopted in his youth by his uncle Antonius Pius, who in turn had been adopted by the Emperor Hadrian, thereby making Marcus an heir to the throne of Rome.

Emperor Marcus Aurelius is sometimes referred to as the last of the 'Five Good Emperors', a phrase first coined by the Italian renaissance writer and philosopher Niccolò Machiavelli. Marcus Aurelius was already a highly successful politician and statesman when he acceded to the throne of Rome in 161 and remained emperor until his death in 180.

Marcus' reign as emperor was characterized by crises and upheavals in the Roman Empire; almost immediately he was faced with wars and uprisings on different fronts. Despite limited experience of battle, Marcus proved to be a great military strategist and a shrewd diplomat. In addition to the almost constant military conflicts, Marcus Aurelius' reign as emperor was also beset with natural disasters. The River Tiber burst its banks, flooding Rome and leading to a famine; a series of earthquakes in the Greek provinces of the empire caused large-scale death and destruction; and the Antonine Plague of 165, believed to be a smallpox pandemic, spread throughout the Roman Empire, claiming the lives of an estimated 10 million people, including Marcus' brother and co-ruler Lucius Verus.

Despite these trials, adversities and personal tragedies (several of Marcus' children died in their infancy), Marcus Aurelius was an extremely popular emperor, revered by his people for his oratorical skills and sound political judgements as much as for his military exploits. He was popular with his fellow statesmen in the senate as well, since he carefully delegated responsibility and promoted openness and trust. Marcus would often ask the senate for permission to spend his considerable personal wealth and regularly stated that the robes of office that he wore and the palaces he resided in belonged to the people of Rome, not to him alone.

Marcus Aurelius mentions Epictetus several times throughout his *Meditations* and had a copy of one of the early editions of Epictetus' *Discourses*. It is thought that there were eight books of Epictetus' *Discourses* but only four survived from antiquity so Marcus was fortunate enough to have read some of Epictetus' teachings, sadly now lost in time.

Marcus Aurelius was highly educated, having been tutored as a young man by several of the finest minds in Roman intellectual life. He developed an interest in Greek literature and philosophy at an early age and at some point was given a copy of Epictetus' *Discourses*. This had a profound effect upon the development of his Stoicism.

As a philosopher, Marcus Aurelius is best known for his *Meditations*, a series of twelve books containing his thoughts and ideas about virtue, duty and spirituality.

The *Meditations* are addressed to himself and were seemingly not intended to ever be published, but just to act as guidance, consolation and practical advice for his own self-improvement and spiritual wellbeing.

Widely regarded as one of the masterpieces of ancient philosophy, the *Meditations* have influenced the lives and thoughts of figures such as John Stuart Mill, Matthew Arnold, Frederick the Great of Prussia and US President Bill Clinton.

PART TWO

THE ART OF LIVING WELL

Practical Stoicism for everyday life

Chapter Three

The Pillars
of Stoicism

You are the one who knows yourself ... you know
how much you are worth in your own estimation
and therefore at what price you sell yourself.[13]

Discourses – Epictetus, Book I, Chapter 2

---

13 Epictetus, *Discourses*, p9

The quotation on the previous page is taken from a chapter in the *Discourses* in which Epictetus discusses how a person can preserve their proper character in any situation. In many passages in the *Discourses* Epictetus uses imaginary conversations to frame his arguments, and in this instance he imagines two people discussing if it is intolerable to be a *latrinarius* or attendant in a public toilet. One person may accept the role for fear of sanction or punishment, and so they will find the job tolerable because they will be free from suffering. Or the same person could accept the role because they need money for food and shelter in order to survive, in which case they would find it tolerable out of necessity. On the other hand, somebody else may reject the role as they consider it beneath their dignity to engage in such demeaning activity. Epictetus dismisses this last judgement as he argues that it adds an additional factor to the question, namely, what is the value of their dignity or sense of self-worth? Instead of worrying about that, the Stoic would accept the situation was tolerable as it was the only situation confronting them in that moment. Resilience and reason would preserve their true character:

'Man, the rational animal can put up with anything except what seems to him to be irrational; whatever is rational is tolerable.'[14]

The Stoics placed great emphasis on character. Here,

---

14 Ibid., p8

character does not mean an individual's personality traits such as their sense of humour or if they are introverts or extroverts, friendly or aloof, but the moral and ethical codes by which they live their life. In this chapter we shall examine the nature of the Stoic notion of character and the four pillars on which Stoicism is based.

The four pillars can be used as a visualization exercise. Try to imagine the four towering, elegant, marble Doric columns that supported the roof of the *Stoa Poikile*, the 'Painted Porch' in the Ancient Agora of Athens, where the foundations of Stoic thought and practice were built.

1. LIVING WITH ARETĒ: BEING YOUR BEST SELF

The art of living is more like wrestling than dancing in that it stands ready for what comes and is not thrown by the unforeseen.[15]

Meditations - Marcus Aurelius, Book VII

---

15 Marcus Aurelius, *Meditations*, p67

In ancient Greece, the term *aretē* was originally used to mean 'excellence' and was liberally applied to anything that was considered of superior quality or value. It could be used to describe things as varied as an athlete at the Olympic Games or an excellent wine, with the meaning modified according to the context. The word has close links with others such as that for 'aristocracy', whose members, according to the caste system, were considered of superior or excellent bloodline. Aretē was also the Greek goddess of knowledge and virtue, and it is those ideals which closely echo the philosophical concept of *aretē* that Aristotle proposed and the Stoics adopted.

According to Aristotle, *aretē* means virtue and the cultivation of excellence in human life. The Stoics took this concept of *aretē* and developed it to mean striving to be the best version of ourselves by following a set of core values and principles. This is a lofty ambition and not something that is suddenly achieved or acquired. On the contrary, it is a lifelong project, a process that needs to be practised, not an end product in and of itself. In order to set off on our journey of living with *aretē*, we must resolve to be our best self in the here and now, and not become distracted or encumbered by what the Stoics termed 'externals' – factors and aspects in our lives that are beyond our control.

Did You Know?

The Romans developed a highly sophisticated drainage and sewage system which included public toilets usually situated near public baths, market places or public squares. Naturally, in a culture that obsessed about health and cleanliness, each public toilet required an attendant known as the *latrinarius*. Far from being merely cleaners or caretakers, a *latrinarius* was quite a skilled position that demanded an intricate knowledge of the workings of the sewage system so they could perform necessary maintenance and upkeep - rather like a modern-day plumber. Nonetheless, the work was usually undertaken by slaves or people of low standing in Roman society.

If living with *aretē* is to cultivate virtue with the goal of living an excellent life, what constitutes virtue? The Stoics very helpfully created a taxonomy of virtue by breaking it down into four main branches: wisdom, courage, justice and temperance. Each one of these cardinal virtues has a natural opposite, a cardinal sin that leads to living with *kakia*[16] – vice and moral bankruptcy.

WISDOM

The Stoics defined wisdom as appropriate responses to situations after careful thought and action. Wisdom is the application of reason but also encompasses common sense, sound judgement, discretion and creativity in the choices that we make. The opposite of wisdom is recklessness, irrationality and selfishness.

COURAGE

In the Stoic view, courage is how we react to adversity and face our fears. Courage encompasses qualities such as perseverance, fortitude, resilience and self-confidence. The opposite of courage is cowardice and weakness of spirit.

---

16   Kakia was also the name of the Greek goddess of sin and vice. She was often depicted as an obese woman indulging in gluttony and sexual impropriety – she was the counter to the goddess Aretē.

JUSTICE

Justice is defined as the way we behave towards other people and the choices we make in our relations with others. Justice is about fairness and generosity, kindness and acting with integrity. The opposite of justice is, unsurprisingly, injustice, along with inequality, prejudice and discrimination.

TEMPERANCE

The Stoics defined temperance as the capacity to exercise self-control, particularly with regard to our emotions and desires, especially negative desires such as anger and lust. Temperance requires our reactions to be disciplined and calm, and embraces aspects such as modesty and forgiveness. Its opposite is lack of control.

As stated previously, living with *aretē* is a process. An individual doesn't just wake up one day and suddenly achieve excellence. One troubling aspect for most people when reflecting on the values and qualities that underpin our characters is how to assess ourselves objectively. No doubt most people like to think that they are essentially kind and have a sense of what is fair and just, but perhaps we are less aware of our emotional responses, particularly our faculties of self-discipline and temperance. Unfortunately, Stoics do not allow for the cherry-picking of virtues: the four branches of wisdom, courage, justice and temperance come as a complete package and need to be practised as a whole and in harmony with each other according to the demands of life.

In addition to being a politician and philosopher, Seneca was also a poet and dramatist of considerable renown. Seneca's dramas fell into obscurity in the early Middle Ages until they were rediscovered by the Italian renaissance writer, Giovanni Boccaccio, author of *The Decameron*. Boccaccio contended that Seneca the philosopher and Seneca the dramatist were two different people. It wasn't until the end of the sixteenth century that scholars were able to prove that the philosopher, politician and playwright were the same person.

If living with *aretē* sounds like a daunting prospect, take inspiration from the following simple lesson from the teachings of Marcus Aurelius:

'When you need encouragement, think of the qualities the people around you have: this one's energy, that one's modesty, another's generosity, and so on. Nothing is as encouraging as when virtues are visibly embodied in the people around us, when we're practically showered with them. It's good to keep this in mind.'[17]

In other words, think about the people that you love and admire, and make a mental list of their virtues. What is it about them that makes them who they are? We encounter many people in our lives with qualities that align with Stoic virtues, but often take them for granted. We may not even realize that we are not recognizing the virtues of others. Perhaps we should. To repeat the words of Marcus Aurelius, 'It's good to keep this in mind.'

---

17 Marcus Aurelius, *Meditations*, p80

2. WHAT DO WE CONTROL?

We are responsible for some things,
while there are other things for which
we cannot be held responsible.[18]

Enchiridion – Epictetus, Chapter I

Thus begins Epictetus' 'Handbook' for Stoic philosophy known as the *Enchiridion*. It is very significant that Arrian, Epictetus' student who scribed and edited Epictetus' thoughts into this manual, should choose as a stepping-off point the statement above, as the question of what we are responsible for is linked to what we can control. Epictetus said that we are responsible for 'our judgement, our impulses, our desires, aversion and mental faculties in general'.[19] The list of things we are not responsible for includes 'the body, material possessions, our reputation, status – in a word anything not in our power of control'.[20]

---

18 Epictetus, *Discourses*, p222

19 Ibid., p221

20 Ibid., p221

Let's examine these distinctions more closely. By 'responsible for', Epictetus means having direct agency over something, that is, total control of it. For example, while we have responsibility for our bodies in terms of following a healthy diet and exercising regularly, we have no control over suddenly getting struck down with illness and disease or being injured in an accident. Similarly, with regard to material possessions, we can take precautions to protect our home, to make it safe and habitable, but we have no control should the water pipes burst and our home is damaged by flooding. In addition, we have no control over how other people view us. We can be civil, take precautions not to deliberately provoke or offend, but ultimately if offence is inadvertently taken we cannot control the emotional reactions of others.

It is tempting to make the distinction that things we can control are inside us, our thoughts and our reactions, and things that we cannot control are external to us. But although Stoics speak a lot about 'externals' and the impermanence of things in the material world, it isn't quite correct that we have total mastery of all our thoughts and actions.

Epictetus says that aspects of our mental impulses which we do have control over are the judgements that we come to and thought processes that influence those judgements. The factors that influence our judgements are 'naturally free, unconstrained and unimpeded', while the factors beyond our control are 'frail, inferior and subject to restraint'.[21]

Epictetus believed therefore that judgements made on the basis of 'externals' beyond our control lead to discontentment and unhappiness, whereas if we 'have the right idea about what really belongs to you and what does not, you will never be subject to force or hindrance'.[22] Put another way, if the desire for material wealth, professional ambitions or to be physically

---

21 Ibid., p221

22 Ibid., p221

attractive consumes a person's judgements, then they are effectively giving control of their future happiness to factors they cannot control. When we free our mind of the weight of external factors we are free to choose our happiness on our own terms.

Another way of looking at judgements (we shall look in more depth at how to discipline our judgements in Chapter Four) is to embrace the idea that when situations beyond our control impact upon our lives, the only responsibility we have is to decide how we wish to react to them. To take an everyday example, perhaps a train you wish to travel on is late or cancelled. You might be on your way to work, or for an important meeting or job interview, but there is nothing in this situation you can directly control – you cannot make the train run on time. Do you rush outside the station and try to hail a taxi? The chances are many other people in your predicament will be doing the same, and there is no guarantee that the traffic will not be heavy and you won't get stuck in a traffic jam. Imagine your stress levels rising, the tension and worry getting worse, all due to a situation over which you have no control. Alternatively, you could telephone the office and explain your misfortune and ask to reschedule the meeting or interview, then buy yourself a coffee and wait for the next train. The time waiting could be spent quietly reflecting on the situation or observing what is happening around you. This would be the Stoic response, to view an unfortunate situation as an opportunity for positive practice. Ah, but what if it isn't possible to reschedule the interview or meeting? Well, Epictetus would simply say that situation is also beyond your control.

To have the wisdom to control our reactions can be difficult, and just like embracing *aretē*, it requires practice and patience as an enduring process. Epictetus does provide some guidance in his 'Handbook'. In order to reap the rewards from the effort, he states that it is necessary to sacrifice other motivations at times and cautions that 'casual effort is not sufficient'.[23]

Bill Belichick, five-time Super Bowl-winning coach of the New England Patriots, puts the enduring success of his team down to his adoption of Stoicism. Belichick discovered Stoicism through the modern Stoic writer Ryan Haliday's books, *The Obstacle is the Way* and *Ego is the Enemy*.

23   Ibid., p221

Epictetus uses the term 'impressions' to explain a cognitive reaction to something external that stimulates thoughts and provokes our responses: 'Make a practice of saying to every strong impression, "An impression is all you are, not the source of the impression."' Epictetus then suggests that we should assess and evaluate the impression with the primary question: 'Is this something that is, or is not, in my control?' And if it is not one of the things that you control be ready with the reaction: 'Then it is not my concern.'[24]

Although we are free to determine our responses to the 'impressions' we encounter, it is important also to accept that we don't always have control over the outcomes. One of the early Athenian Stoics, Antipater of Tarsus (died *c*.130 BC), is credited with introducing the metaphor of the archer to describe the Stoic attitude to misfortune. A crack archer, through skill and practice, can train themselves to hit their target

24   Ibid., p222

ten times out of ten; eventually, however, the archer will miss. This is not because of negligence on the archer's part: a sudden gust of wind could blow the arrow off course or their bowstring may snap at the crucial point. These are factors beyond the archer's control. What is important, according to Antipater, is that the archer accepts the misfortune, consoled with the knowledge that they had done the best they possibly could in unfortunate circumstances.

3. TAKING RESPONSIBILITY AND ASKING THE RIGHT QUESTIONS

Do not imagine that, if something is hard for you to achieve, it is therefore impossible for any man; but rather consider anything that is humanly possible and appropriate to lie within your own reach too.[25]

Meditations – Marcus Aurelius, Book VI

25   Marcus Aurelius, *Meditations*, p50

When Stoics speak of responsibility they are referring to a specific idea of morality which states that we alone are responsible for our actions, and it is our duty to act according to virtue – to try to be and do good. As discussed previously, what we are responsible for is what is 'up to us', things that we can control.

To return to Epictetus' idea of 'impressions' as something external that provides stimulus, how we respond to this stimulus is determined by the judgements we make, judgements which we are free to make. There is a short space of time after the impression (stimulus) during which we can formulate our response (judgement), but too often our responses are instinctive reactions coloured by unconscious and possibly negative assumptions. In order to try to have mastery over our judgements, the Stoic practice is to inhabit that space that exists between initial stimulus and response, to step back and question if our response is reasoned and appropriate or if it is irrational and impulsive.

Marcus Aurelius writes about freeing ourselves of our innate assumptions and kneejerk reactions: 'Today

I escaped from all bothering circumstances – or rather I threw them out. They were nothing external, but inside me, just my own judgements.'[26]

By withholding our assent to how we initially or instinctively respond to a situation or circumstance, we escape the threat of thoughtless and impetuous reactions, which are damaging to our emotional and mental wellbeing. 'Remove your judgements whenever you wish and then there is calm – as the sailor rounding the cape finds smooth water and the welcome of a waveless bay,'[27] states Marcus Aurelius, using an elegant metaphor of the mind as a boat seeking serene waters to sail in.

There are of course certain situations where our responses to impressions provoke instinctive reactions, which, in the heat of the moment, are impossible to withhold assent from. Emotional responses that

26 Ibid., p87
27 Ibid., p119

provoke tears and grief, or an adrenalin rush through fear or danger leading to a quickening of the pulse or a pounding heartbeat, are naturally intuitive bodily responses that are difficult to control at the time. In these situations, what is important is how we react to these impulses afterwards. Were we able to still the beating heart or throbbing vein? After the initial impulse, were we able to make a positive judgement on an appropriate outcome?

4. NURTURING *EUDAIMONIA*

Dig inside yourself. Inside there is a spring of goodness ready to gush at any moment, if you keep digging.[28]

Meditations – Marcus Aurelius, Book VII

The concept of *eudaimonia* was first coined by Aristotle in his work *Nichomachean Ethics*. The basic translation of the Greek word is 'happiness', although this is not quite right in this philosophical case. Aristotle defines

---

28   Ibid., p67

eudaimonia not as a state of mind or a fleeting feeling of pleasure, gratification or contentment, as happiness is often thought to be, but as the highest human good, the only human good that is desirable for its own sake (as an end in itself) rather than for the sake of something else (as a means to achieve some other end result or goal).

Did You Know?

Nichomachean Ethics was part of Aristotle's quest to create a science of happiness and probably developed from his teachings at his school in Athens, the Lyceum. The title of the work and what it refers to is never revealed in the text. Some scholars argue that Aristotle may have dictated the text to his son, whose name was Nichomachus, and who took over as head of the Lyceum after Aristotle's death. However, Nichomachus was also the name of Aristotle's father (it was a Greek tradition to name children after their grandfathers). One neat interpretation is that *Nichomachean Ethics* gives the guiding principles of how to live a life of virtue, passed down through the generations of Aristotle's family, from grandfather to son and on to grandchild.

The Stoics took Aristotle's concept of *eudaimonia* as the highest human good and interpreted it as the highest or best version of oneself. The Greeks believed that there was a divine spirit planted inside every living person in the form of a *daimon*, a personification of the human condition. Broken down, *eu* means good and *daimon*, a spirit guide in the form of a moral compass, so to nurture *eudaimonia* was to foster a good *daimon* and hence to live well. The Stoics believed that the guiding forces of nature desire that we live in harmony with nature itself, and we should strive to be the best we can, living our best life that is smooth-flowing and free from troubles and strife either internally or externally.

So by living a life guided by reason and in accordance with nature we can hope to narrow the gap between our potential best self and the person that we actually are. As with many Stoic ideas, achieving *eudaimonia* does not suddenly happen; it is a process, and progress towards that goal of living well brings its own rewards. For example, it helps build resilience to deal with the judgements that we make and any misfortunes that may befall us.

The Pillars of Stoicism

As we have seen in this chapter, the principles of Stoicism are closely entwined with the concept of the Stoic character. We can develop the Stoic character needed to nurture *eudaimonia* and live our best life by several means: by living with *aretē*, striving to be the best version of ourselves through the cultivation of the virtues of wisdom, courage, justice and temperance; by distinguishing what we can and cannot control; and by taking responsibility for our responses, actions and judgements.

Where the Stoics and Aristotle differ is in their view of the impact that external aspects have in our pursuit of living our best life and nurturing *eudaimonia*. In *Nichomachean Ethics*, Aristotle appears to break down *eudaimonia* to three components of goodness: goodness of the soul (our virtues, including courage, wisdom, generosity of spirit, etc.); goodness of the body (our physical health); and the goodness of external things (wealth, power and influence). Aristotle takes a pragmatic view of the goodness of externals and argues that human beings, rightly or wrongly, live in communities where our lives are constrained and conditioned by factors such as wealth, political power and relationships, and that certain virtuous practices are likewise subject to constraints. For example, it would be impossible to be generous and show kindness to the poor and dispossessed without the resources to do so. Similarly, if we want to effect change in society, to live in a free and more equal world, we will need to wield political influence and seek the support of others.

The Stoics however, reject the view that our happiness can be determined to any degree by external goods, which they label as 'indifferents', things which are neither good nor bad in themselves and whose presence or absence holds no bearing on our happiness. Stoics hold that the exercise of virtue is the only expression of true happiness and the pathway to *eudaimonia*.

Marcus Aurelius seems to warn against including externals in our view of how to live a happy and virtuous life when he writes: 'Happiness is a benign god or a divine blessing, why then, my imagination, are you doing what you are doing? Go away ... I have no need of you. You have come in your old habit.'[29] In other words, we may imagine that wealth and prosperity may make us happy, but more often than not, the opposite is true. A truly virtuous life is enough for happiness and nurturing *eudaimonia*.

Likewise, as Seneca writes to his friend Lucilius: 'The supreme ideal [*eudaimonia*] does not call for any external aids. It is home-grown, wholly self-developed. Once it starts looking outside itself for any part of

---

29   Ibid., p65

itself it is on the way to being dominated by fortune.'[30] Or it might be prone to forces and factors beyond our control.

Nature designed the mind to assent to what is true, dissent from what is false and suspend judgement in doubtful cases. Similarly, it conditioned the mind to desire what is good, to reject what is bad and to regard with indifference what is neither one nor the other.[31]

Discourses – Epictetus, Book 3

30 Seneca, *Letters from a Stoic*, p51

31 Epictetus, *Discourses*, p147

Chapter Four

The Discipline of Judgement

Remove the judgement and you have removed the thought 'I am hurt': remove the thought 'I am hurt', and the hurt itself is removed.[32]

Meditations – Marcus Aurelius, Book IV

---

32 Marcus Aurelius, *Meditations*, p25

Many people spend their life worrying about things. They worry about their finances, about their work, about the result of previous actions and future outcomes; in short, they worry about perceived problems in their life. The definition of a problem is something which is considered to be injurious or detrimental to living a contented life. However things are only problems if we consider them to be so and it is precisely in this considered judgement that the sense of worry lies.

> Many famous authors have cited Marcus Aurelius as a major influence upon their work including Harry Potter creator J. K. Rowling, who cites the emperor philosopher as someone who 'will never let you down' when in need of a wise word.

Epictetus recognized that 'it is not events that disturb people, it is their judgements concerning them'.[33] As we have seen, we can only control certain things

---

33 Epictetus, *Discourses*, p223

and we should reject concerns over matters beyond our control. Thankfully our judgements are within the realm of things we can control. The question therefore is, how can we train our minds to make better judgements about things in the world around us? The Stoics call this process and practice the discipline of assent or the discipline of judgement.

DON'T BE TOO QUICK TO JUDGE

Reason wishes that the judgement it gives be just; anger wishes that the judgement it has given seem to be just.[34]

'On a Happy Life' (*De Vita Beata*) - Seneca the Younger

---

34 Seneca, *Dialogues and Essays*, trans. Davie, John, Oxford University Press, Oxford, 2008, pp85–112

For Stoics, the discipline of assent is the process through which our minds form value judgements. Assent is taken to mean 'to be in agreement with' or 'to be in accord with'. This process, if practised correctly, takes the form of a type of Stoic mindfulness that can be applied to everyday situations.

One of the follies of our judgements is to be reactive, to leap to snap judgements in the moment. Take, for example, an incident of road rage. Suppose a person is driving to work one morning during rush hour when another driver cuts in front of them at a roundabout and infringes their right of way. The infringement causes the person to instantly slam on the brakes to avoid an accident which could cause injury to themselves and their vehicle. This incident creates an 'impression' of danger and risk of harm. The mind of the driver assents to this impression and reacts accordingly. However, what happens next may be an involuntary and unconscious snap reaction in the form of a value judgement. The driver may aggressively honk their horn, shout expletives and insults, or make offensive gestures. The person has therefore succumbed to assent to a negative judgement that is now causing them psychological and physical distress. Their heartbeat has quickened, their pulse is racing, and their face is flushed red with rage. The person's response is not at all uncommon, but it is fostering unwanted anguish and stress upon themselves.

The Stoic response to such a situation is to apply reason and practical wisdom to negate snap value judgements that are harmful to physical and mental wellbeing. This is achieved by a three-step approach known as 'Stop', 'Strip' and 'See'.

STOP: The first step involved is stopping the negative reaction in its tracks by suspending value judgements – think of it as a type of mental cease and desist order. To return to our road-rage incident, this should have occurred the moment the driver slammed on the brakes. There are various ways that we can stop our reactions to things before they take a grip, like holding our breath and counting slowly to ten.

STRIP or LAY BARE: The next step involves seeing the incident for what it is and applying what in psychotherapy terms is known as 'decatastrophizing' – describing what just happened in plain terms free from emotion. For example: 'Another driver was driving without due care and attention'. Once we have in our mind a plain description, stripped of emotional or inflammatory language, we can better evaluate the impression and see through it.

SEE: The third step involves seeing the situation from a wider perspective or alternative perspectives, then questioning and evaluating it. What was the worst that could have happened? The person driving recklessly could have caused serious injury, even death. Is it possible to control how someone else drives? No, it is beyond our control. Did the person deliberately drive recklessly? Were they even aware that they were driving recklessly? Perhaps they were stressed and in a hurry. By asking and answering questions we are able to come to judgements based upon reason, and not make snap decisions which may have negative outcomes.

The early Greek Stoic philosopher Chrysippus had an unusual name - a combination of the ancient Greek words: Chrysos, meaning gold; and hippos meaning horse, therefore the third Scholarch (head of school) of Stoicism was nicknamed the Golden Horse.

Epictetus mentions 'challenges' that must be overcome in his handbook, advising that 'for every challenge remember the resources you have within you to cope with it' and promises that with practice 'in time, you will grow to be confident that there is not a single impression that you will not have the moral means to tolerate'.[35]

Epictetus alludes to how to deal with people who affront others with rudeness or ill-manners, writing that even if we feel a sense of injury, we should pull back from forming judgements on such impressions. He argues that 'if you are insulted you will discover patience'.[36]

Similarly Marcus Aurelius opens his second book of *Meditations* by counselling the following:

'Say to yourself first thing in the morning: today I shall meet people who are meddling, ungrateful, aggressive, treacherous, malicious, unsocial. All this

---

35   Ibid., p225

36   Ibid., p225

has afflicted them through their ignorance of true good and evil.'[37]

He then goes on to argue that as he has 'seen the nature of good is what is right and the nature of evil is what is wrong' he cannot be harmed by others' insults and rudeness, for the only harm it does is to the offender as 'to work in opposition to each other is against nature ... and anger and rejection is opposition'.[38]

WALKING IN OTHER PEOPLE'S SHOES

Accustom yourself not to be disregarding of what someone else has to say: as far as possible enter into the mind of the speaker.[39]

Meditations – Marcus Aurelius, Book VI

Developing good listening skills and becoming a good listener are tools in a Stoic's box. Marcus Aurelius advises us to listen carefully to what is being said to

---

37 Marcus Aurelius, *Meditations*, p10

38 Ibid., p10

39 Ibid., p57

us in any given moment and not dismiss things out of hand without first carefully reflecting upon the words. What impression are the words causing us? Do we need to pull back from making a rash judgement as to their meaning? Marcus Aurelius expands this approach to include trying to enter into the mind of the speaker. Not literally, of course – not by attempting telepathy or paranormal projection – but through carefully reflecting on the way someone says something and what their motivations are, and trying to see things from their perspective. This is akin to the old saying 'walk a mile in someone else's shoes before you judge them'.

Did You Know?

The well-known proverb, often mistakenly attributed to various Native American tribes, 'to take time to walk a mile in their moccasins', is actually derived from the poem 'Judge Softly' by Mary T. Lathrap (1838–95) which was published posthumously. She was a white Methodist preacher, writer and activist from Michigan who campaigned for causes as varied as universal suffrage and prohibition. The poem contains several references to the lives of Native Americans on the reservations, so it may have been inspired by their plight, and it has clear echoes of the Stoic principles of fostering empathy and developing a discipline of judgement:

Just walk a mile in his moccasins
Before you abuse, criticize and accuse.
If just for one hour, you could find a way
To see through his eyes, instead of your
own muse.

'Judge Softly' – Mary T. Lathrop (1895)

Empathy is extremely powerful, and by trying to put ourselves in the mind of the speaker, or 'walking in their shoes', we are practising an important skill that will be of benefit to healthy interactions and relationships. Marcus Aurelius believes that 'in conversation one ought to follow closely what is said, in any impulse what takes place. In the latter case, to see immediately the intended object of reference: in the former, to watch carefully what is meant'.[40] These are powerful words. Think of all the petulant gripes, peevish distresses and sullen sulks caused by casual words and simple misunderstandings that could have been avoided if someone had just listened properly. By considering not only the meaning of the words being spoken or the actions and impulses they provoke, but also evaluating the thoughts and emotions from which those impressions have sprung, we can form stronger bonds with people.

---

40   Ibid., pp58–9

Marcus Aurelius also has advice for when we may feel that perhaps the intention behind the action or words has been harsh or unjust. Taking Plato's assertion that 'no soul likes to be deprived of the truth', he argues that 'the same also holds for justice, moderation, kindness and all such virtues. Essential that you should keep this constantly in your mind: this will make you gentler to all'.[41] He is encouraging us to reflect inwardly on the goodness of virtue and to make a choice as to how we react to a perceived slight or injury. Perhaps the perpetrator did so without feeling or proper thought, in which case the problem is theirs, not yours. If they acted out of premeditated malice then again the problem is most certainly theirs. As the children's rhyme goes: sticks and stones can break our bones but words can never hurt us – unless we judge them to.

41 Ibid., p67

FOSTER EMPATHY, NOT BLAME

The sign of a person making progress:
they never criticize, praise, blame or
point the finger, or represent their self as
knowing or amounting to anything. If they
experience frustration or disappointment
they point the finger at themselves.[42]

Enchiridion – Epictetus, Chapter 48

As discussed, the discipline of walking in other
people's shoes is key in developing an empathetic
character. Epictetus suggests that acting with humility
is also a sign of progress towards living with *aretē*
and nurturing *eudaimonia*, two of the pillars on which
Stoic wisdom is based. When Epictetus writes that
people shouldn't portray themselves as 'knowing or
amounting to anything' he is echoing Plato's *Apology*, in
which Socrates states his view of wisdom as knowing
that he knows nothing. By this Socrates isn't literally
confessing ignorance, since by most measures Socrates
was one of the wisest people who ever lived. What he

---

42   Epictetus, *Discourses*, p242

was actually stating was a refusal to adopt a hubristic attitude towards knowledge, one which blithely states 'I am right and you are wrong'. For Epictetus a 'blame game' is a similar folly, for it supposes our frustrations or disappointments are the responsibility of others and not ourselves. Hence the wise person points the finger not at others but at themselves. Their judgement is not coloured by self-righteous anger or the fury of perceived injustice, but by the wisdom of humility: 'An ignorant person is inclined to blame others for his own misfortune. To blame oneself is proof of progress.'[43]

Humility helps to foster empathy because it seeks to disarm conflicts and divisions between people. Marcus Aurelius believed we should also recognize and embrace the inter-connectedness of all things as a foil against disunion and strife: 'Think always of the universe as one living creature, comprising one substance and one

---

43   Ibid., p223

soul: how all is absorbed into this one consciousness.'[44] The rationale is that all things in the universe are parts of one infinite whole, and human beings are physically part of the whole because of our physical substance, and metaphysically part of the whole because of our souls. If we are all absorbed into this 'one consciousness' we are at one with everything in nature, so we can empathize because we are all part of the whole.

After the Emperor Hadrian became Marcus Aurelius' adoptive grandfather, certain privileges were bestowed upon the young Marcus, including being admitted to the College of Salii, an exclusive sect of priests. The Salii were a group of twelve boy warriors, who were dedicated to Mars the God of War. Known as 'the leaping priests', the Salii wore a uniform and performed acrobatic dance routines with shields and spears at rituals and festivals in Mars' honour and on feast days.

---

44 Marcus Aurelius, *Meditations*, p31

This is a powerful idea, the notion that we are a part of a bigger entity and so therefore connected to all things, yet it is an important step in fostering empathy and compassion.

SEEING THINGS AS THEY ARE

The only safe harbour in this life's tossing troubled sea is to refuse to be bothered about what the future will bring and to stand ready and confident, squaring the breast without skulking or flinching whatever fortune hurls at us.[45]

Moral Epistles to Lucilius – Seneca, Letter 94

How often do we find ourselves consumed with anxiety about future events or situations, worrying ourselves witless about what may or may not come to pass? Seneca returns to this problem several times in his letters to his friend Lucilius. In Letter 13 he writes 'How often has the unexpected happened! How often has the

---

45 Seneca, *Letters from a Stoic*, p190

expected never come to pass!'[46] He observes that 'some
things torment us more than they ought; some torment
us before they ought; and some torment us when they
ought not to torment us at all. We are in the habit of
exaggerating, or imagining, or anticipating, sorrow.'[47]

Seneca's point is that we become so wrapped up with
the crippling cramps of apprehension that we can't 'see
the wood for the trees', or put another way, we can't 'see
things as they are'.

Seneca's 'safe harbour' can seem a distant, unreachable
sanctuary at times. Stoics don't pretend that life is easy
and just wave away misfortune with a dismissive shrug
and a weary sigh. At Stoicism's core is developing a way of
looking at the world unencumbered by mental baggage
– much of which is irrational, harmful and detrimental
to our peace of mind. Certainly it takes resilience to

---

46 Seneca, *Moral Epistles to Lucilius*, trans. Gummere, Richard M,
Heineman, London, 1917 – Letter 13 'On Groundless Fear'

47 Ibid.

'square up' to adversity and not be constantly fearing the future, fretting over what may or may not happen. Instead Stoics concentrate on the present as the only way to see things as they are, not how they were, or how they could be.

In an episode of the popular science fiction television series *Doctor Who*, the Doctor's assistant Clara Oswald (played by Jenna Coleman) quotes Marcus Aurelius' memorable line to a classroom of teenagers: 'Waste no more time arguing what a good man should be. Be one.'

This takes the exercise of one of the four virtues, wisdom. Seneca writes to Lucilius in Letter 64 how he contemplates the exercise of wisdom with a mixture of bafflement and awe, and yet gives a handy tip for how we can practise trying to 'see things as they are': 'I gaze upon her [wisdom] with bewilderment, just as I sometimes gaze upon the firmament itself, which I often behold as if I saw it for the first time.'[48]

Thus Seneca's technique for 'seeing things as they are' is to imagine his mind is seeing the world as if he's never seen it before. Many of our anxieties are repeated over and over so they become all too familiar. In a sense, it is precisely because we are acquainted with 'sorrow' (Seneca uses the word sorrow to denote any mental anguish, which could range from grief to anxiety to depression) that we find ourselves trapped in to a cycle. But imagine for a moment, if we were to step away, metaphorically, and look upon an issue or a situation as if we were experiencing it for the first time, our perception of it would be clearer for we would be viewing it in the present and not concerning ourselves with our past sufferings or possible future outcomes.

The Stoics acknowledged that our imagination has an effect upon us psychologically and this in turn impacts

---

48   Ibid., Letter 64 'On The Philosopher's Task' [6]

upon our mental wellbeing and our behaviour. Our perception of the world around us and our sense of self can be heavily affected and this can lead to self-delusions. This is the danger of literally overthinking situations – trying to predict outcomes or prepare our responses in advance of some perceived calamity.

The Stoics suggest that our anxieties and worries, that feeling of sickness and dread in the pit of the stomach, arise from this negative use of our imaginative faculties, yet conversely this can be controlled through exercising self-control and discipline in our judgements, and in doing so developing our capacity for resilience.

There are more things, Lucilius, likely to frighten us than there are to crush us; we suffer more often in imagination than in reality.[49]

Moral Epistles to Lucilius – Seneca, Letter 13

---

49   Ibid., Letter 13 'On Groundless Fear' [4]

The Discipline of Judgement

In this chapter we have explored the Stoic concept of the discipline of judgement. We have seen how easy it is to be too quick to judge situations, to instinctively respond without properly evaluating the circumstances. To this end the three-step approach of Stop, Strip, and See provides a useful framework to help us avoid making snap judgements or reactions, and allows us time to reflect.

We have also discussed how important it is to try to 'walk in other people's shoes' – to see situations and motivations from another perspective. This will involve developing empathy and strong listening skills. Crates of Thebes, the forefather of Stoicism, had a reputation as an excellent listener, which is one reason why people would welcome him to their homes and have him advise on their problems and disputes (see Chapter One). By fostering empathy we are able to strengthen the bonds between us and negate the forces that seek to divide us. And finally we have discussed seeing things as they are, not how they might have been in the past or fretting about how they may be in the future, but how they actually are in the here and now.

Chapter Five

The Discipline
of Emotions

The question has often been raised whether it
is better to have moderate emotions, or none
at all. Philosophers of our school reject the
emotions; the Peripatetics keep them in check.
I, however, do not understand how any halfway
disease can be either wholesome or helpful.[50]

Moral Epistles to Lucilius – Seneca, Letter 116

---

50   Ibid., Letter 116 'On Self Control'

One of the misconceptions of Stoicism (as discussed in the introduction) is that it is a school of thought that encourages people to repress their emotions, to become unfeeling automatons programmed not to react and just to 'take it on the chin'. Seneca, in a letter to Lucilius quoted above, appears at face value to suggest that 'our school reject the emotions' – that Stoics do believe in suppressing emotive responses. The contrasting position Seneca cites is of the Peripatetics (followers of Aristotle) who advocate controlling emotion through the application of reason, keeping emotions 'in check'. Seneca, however, rejects this position too, arguing that to accept emotions as inevitable and try to mitigate their negative consequences is a form of unnecessary crisis management. It would be much better then, from a Stoic perspective, not to deny, nor try to control our emotions in certain situations, but rather to try to not have them at all. In this chapter we shall discuss how we can tame our emotional impulses and develop strategies of self-control and resilience.

NEGATIVE THOUGHTS BREED NEGATIVE OUTCOMES

In order to fully grasp the Stoic view of emotions it is necessary to apply the opposing concepts of *pathē* and *eupatheiai*. The former, closely linked to *pathos* in Greek tragedy, encompasses negative emotional reactions such as anger, fear, envy, hatred and shame. The latter encompasses positive emotional reactions such as compassion, friendliness, love and joy. Or put simply, *pathē* equals 'bad vibes' and *'eupatheiai'* equals 'good vibes'.

When Seneca speaks of emotions he is usually referring exclusively to negative passions, i.e. *pathē*. In his essay 'On Anger', Seneca writes about what he terms as 'first movements' – our initial, instinctive responses to an emotive stimulus:

'...the first movement is involuntary, and is, as it were, a preparation for a passion, and a threatening of one. The next is combined with a wish, though not an obstinate one, as, for example, "It is my duty to avenge myself, because I have been injured," or "It is right that this man should be punished, because he has committed a crime." The third emotion is already beyond our control, because it overrides reason, and wishes to avenge itself.'[51]

There are therefore three stages or movements in our emotive responses that could result in *pathē*. The first movement is pure instinct, and Seneca argues it is a natural response which is no more avoidable than suppressing a yawn when somebody else yawns in your company. What is important is what happens next as we progress from the first movement to the second or third. Seneca suggests that after the initial instinctive reaction, the mind responds to that emotional jolt by forming a judgement. As discussed in the previous chapter, if we apply discipline in the formation of our judgements we take control of

51 Seneca, *Minor Dialogues Together with the Dialogue 'On Clemency',* trans. Stewart, Aubrey; pp.76–114. Bohn's Classical Library Edition; George Bell and Sons, London, 1900 – Wikisource 'On Anger' (*De Ira*) Book I Ch IV

them. If, however, we allow our initial reactions to gather momentum and develop into destructive emotions we will surrender control and will be lurching towards the third movement which 'overrides reason'.

It is not easy to gain mastery of our emotions, especially in situations where we feel we have been unjustly wronged; when, for example, somebody insults us or criticizes us, seemingly without reason or provocation. Epictetus addresses this problem in the *Enchiridion* when he asserts:

Remember, it is not enough to be hit or insulted to be harmed, you must believe that you are being harmed. If someone succeeds in provoking you, realize that your mind is complicit in the provocation.[52]

So we are only hurt or insulted if we allow ourselves to be, if we are 'complicit in the provocation'. The modern Stoicism writer, John Sellars, has interpreted and extrapolated on Epictetus' ideas in his book *Lessons in Stoicism*.[53]

Sellars suggests that after the initial first movement of hurt or alarm at a perceived slight or criticism, we should consider if there is any validity or truth to the criticism. Should we decide that there is, we may have said or done something thoughtlessly, so we can then

---

52 Epictetus, *Discourses*, p228

53 Sellars, John, *Lessons in Stoicism*, Penguin Random House, London, 2020

address a character flaw or error of judgement of which we were hitherto unaware. If, however, we conclude that there is no legitimacy to the criticism, then it is the other person who is wrong and guilty of poor judgement and exposure to *pathē* – the negative passions of anger, envy, fear and hatred. They are the only person ultimately suffering harm.

Epictetus also suggests a novel method of deflecting and disarming unwarranted criticism or denunciation: 'If you learn that someone is speaking ill of you, don't try to defend yourself against the rumours; respond instead with, "Yes, and he doesn't know the half of it, because he could have said more."'[54] By accepting that we can only be hurt if we assent to being hurt, we maintain control over the situation. Likewise, by adopting a sense of ironic self-deprecation, as Epictetus counsels, we disarm our accusers and expose their folly and ignorance. As Marcus Aurelius observed: 'Mere things, brute facts should

---

54 Epictetus, *Discourses*, p237

not provoke your rage, they have no mind to care.'[55] Circumstances have no care for our feelings and by allowing them to provoke anger we are encouraging *pathē* – bad vibes – and that can only result in one outcome, because negative thoughts breed negative outcomes.

COURAGE AND CALM VERSUS FEAR AND FURY

The Stoic philosophy pivots around the concepts of virtue and living with *aretē* – cultivating virtue with the aim of living to our best. Of the virtues of wisdom, justice, temperance and courage, it is courage that has the most specific definition. We often think of courage in terms of courageous acts – people who have responded to some awful atrocity to help or save the lives of others, or soldiers in times of warfare, selflessly putting their lives on the line for the common good or to protect others. Although these are undoubtedly displays of courage and bravery, the Stoic virtue of courage is more nuanced. Seneca gives a neat definition of the Stoic view of courage when he wrote to his friend Lucilius that 'bravery is not thoughtless rashness, or love of danger, or the courting of fear-inspiring objects; it is the knowledge which enables us to distinguish between that which is evil and that which is not'.

---

55   Marcus Aurelius, *Meditations*, p64

By distinguishing between 'evil' things and things that aren't evil, Seneca is not pointing to the traditional dichotomies such as good versus evil or love versus hate; he is defining evil as anything that has a negative or detrimental effect and impact upon our lives. Courage in this sense is less focused on individual acts of bravery, but more concerned with building the psychological and moral strength to face up to our fears and anxieties about aspects of life that cause us pain and mental distress. Courage as a virtue can be resilience and inner strength in the face of external pressures from the physical, social or psychological spheres.

Marcus Aurelius, a distinguished and fearless soldier and brilliant military strategist, wrote about the human mind and the capacity to summon reserves of resilience in the face of adversity:

'The mind adapts and turns round any obstacle to action to serve its objective: a hindrance to a given work is turned into a furtherance. An obstacle in a given path becomes an advance.'[56]

---

56 Ibid., p42

This notion of turning adversity into an opportunity to improve ourselves is a key cornerstone of Stoic philosophy. Removing the obstacle becomes an objective in itself, a chance to reframe our perceptions of circumstances and conquer fears and anxieties.

A simple example of this proactive approach to obstacles in our lives, things that cause us anxiety or distress, can been seen in how people conquer their phobias through desensitization or self-exposure therapies. For example, I suffer from arachnophobia, a fear of spiders, due in the main to a mildly traumatic experience I had when I was a young child. When I became a father I noticed that my daughter also had this fear, and I began to worry that I had somehow transferred my phobia to her. It seemed unlikely that this was in any way a matter of genetics, since I'm unaware of any other members of my family past or present being frightened of spiders, thus it must be learned behaviour. My daughter must have seen me recoil and sensed my aversion when confronted by a spider and naturally concluded that spiders were evil or dangerous.

So I set about conquering my phobia to show my daughter that it is an irrational and impulsive reaction. I also wanted to rid myself of an obstacle, which although a very minor hindrance in my life, was nonetheless a long-standing cause of random anxiety (See Part Three: Each Day in the Life of a Practising Stoic).

Seneca owned several vineyards and produced his own wine which was considered among the finest in the Roman Empire. In his essay 'On the Tranquillity of Mind' Seneca writes: 'At times we ought to drink even to intoxication, not so as to drown, but merely to dip ourselves in wine: for wine washes away troubles and dislodges them from the depths of the mind, and acts as a remedy to sorrow as it does to some diseases.'

In the end it all comes down to a simple matter of choice: do we choose courage and use resilience and strength to face obstacles and adversities? Or do we choose fear and find ourselves in a state of paralysis, surrendering to negative emotions?

Linked to this decision is a choice concerning our emotional reactions to situations that present obstacles or that we find irksome. Courage in the form of resilience needs self-control, which can only be exerted from a calm mind. It is not possible to act according to reason when one is consumed with rage. As Marcus Aurelius wrote: 'It is the gentle who have strength, sinew and courage – not the indignant and complaining.'[57] Therefore the choice is simple: take stock of the situation, clear the mind of negative thoughts and emotions, and this will calm the mind for 'the closer the control of emotion, the closer the power'.[58]

The Stoic virtue of courage is then about how we deal with problems and issues in our lives. Do we confront them head-on with the view that we can draw strength and resilience from taking that path, or do we bury our head in the sand through fear or self-denial? No matter how complicated a situation may appear, at its heart lies the truth that we can only control what is 'ours' and that is how we choose to respond, with fury and fear, or with courage and calm.

---

57 Ibid., p111

58 Ibid., p111

NEVER ACT ON IMPULSE

We must discover an art of assent, and in the whole field of our impulses, take care to ensure that each impulse is conditional, has a social purpose and is proportionate to the value of its goal.[59]

Meditations – Marcus Aurelius, Book XI

When Marcus Aurelius was a young man, as part of his instruction in the noble science of philosophy he was given a copy of Epictetus' *Discourses*. The book had a profound effect upon his thoughts and he frequently references it in his own *Meditations*. The quote above is Marcus Aurelius paraphrasing the *Discourses* on how best to manage our impulses to action by developing ('discovering') 'an art of assent'. It is essential to note that impulses are akin to the Stoic concept of 'impressions' that in turn provoke 'movements' (responses) which spur actions and reactions. A good example of this chain of events – and an illustration of *eupatheiai* ('good vibes') – is when we run into an

---

59   Ibid., p114

old friend unexpectedly. First the impression caused through recognition, next the movement of surprise followed by the reaction of happiness or pleasure and the action of an embrace. This example shows a natural flow in the process of assent. However, often there is discord and it is here that the initial mental jolt, the impulse, needs to be 'conditional'.

The term 'conditional' here means 'with reservations' – not in the sense of algebra or grammar where there are conditions which need to be satisfied. Hence it is again an instruction to stop and reflect, to weigh up the 'conditions' in which the impulse has been provoked.

Epictetus, in contrast to Seneca and Marcus Aurelius, who were extremely wealthy and priviledged, lived a very modest life. In this respect Epictetus aligned with the *Antipaterist* school of Stoicism that had more in common with the traditional Greek roots of the philosophy and the teachings of the Cynics who advocated asceticism.

The interesting aspect to what Epictetus decreed and Marcus Aurelius interpreted and embraced is the concept of our impulses having a 'social purpose'. This is perhaps harder to assess in terms of modern life which functions and thrives at a furious and often dizzying speed, but it is precisely why we should take the time to reflect upon the possible impact and outcomes of what we assent to as a result of our impulses/impressions. Who gains any benefit or reward from our actions? Is it to the benefit of everyone or just to ourselves? Furthermore, is it 'proportionate to its goal'? That is, are we sure we aren't overreacting, assenting to a course of action before properly thinking things through?

Overreacting to situations is something everyone is guilty of on occasion and is often caused by external factors. Work stresses, anxieties about the future, social and financial pressures, problems with family and friends, physical and mental health issues can all cause people to fly off the handle – like a pressure cooker suddenly exploding. But once we realize we have overreacted it is very rare to feel in any sense vindicated by our response. To just think 'Okay, maybe I overreacted, but I was provoked' is to miss the point and be in denial. The Stoic response is to accept and 'own' the overreaction then reflect and question. We return again to one of the pillars of Stoicism, namely how we can take control and ask the right questions. This can only be achieved through self-reflection.

Seneca, in a letter to his friend Lucilius, writes of his daily practice of self-reflection: 'I shall put myself under observation straight away and undertake a review of my day – a course which is of the utmost benefit.'[60] The value of journalling (keeping a record of your feelings and thoughts) as a mode of self-reflection is discussed in Part Three, but it is worth mentioning here the benefits of looking back on events in relation to overreactions caused by impulse. Seneca continues: 'What really ruins our character is that none of us looks back over his life.'[61] So, in the aftermath of an overreaction, one question to ask is: 'Has a similar situation occurred before?' If so, do you always experience a particular impulse that is prompted by a certain impression? It is possible that you have unearthed something that triggers negative emotions in you, anxieties or frustrations which you can now set aside and put to further examination.

For a Stoic, of course, it would be preferable if the overreaction caused on impulse had never happened in the first place. If the discipline of judgement had been

---

60 Seneca, *Letters from a Stoic*, p141

61 Ibid., p141

appropriately followed (see Chapter Four), then our actions would have been determined by reason and not by emotional impulse. Nonetheless, we are all human, we all have things we don't like, bugbears and gripes, and the important thing is to confront them, not to assent to them and surrender our self-control. This is what Marcus Aurelius is referring to when he says that each impulse is 'conditional'; we need to approach our impulses with reservations, particularly in moments of crisis and strife.

Health and Safety in Ancient Rome

Acrobatic circus shows were a popular form of entertainment in ancient Rome, with trapeze and rope artists and tightrope walkers performing death-defying stunts. The circus troupes were often made up of lithe, young boys whose athleticism was seen as good preparation for military training. According to the Roman historian Cassius Dio, who wrote a mammoth eighty-volume *Roman History* in Greek (*Rhōmaïkè Historía*), Marcus Aurelius attended a performance in which one of the young acrobats fell from the high wire and died. Marcus, who was emperor at the time, was so distressed by the accident that he ordered mattresses to be placed beneath all future aerial performances. He thus developed the first safety net commonly used in circuses ever since.

Cassius Dio also reports that despite being a decorated military hero, Marcus Aurelius had a rather squeamish temperament and ordered that gladiator fights in the Coliseum be undertaken with blunt or wooden swords. Although these weapons were still capable of causing injury, they greatly reduced the probability of death. Many modern historians have also disputed the 'blood and gore' Hollywood depictions of Roman gladiators in film and television dramas, arguing that most gladiators lived relatively long and prosperous lives, had the status of modern rock stars, and were much too valuable a commodity in terms of box office appeal to casually slaughter on a weekly basis. It seems Marcus Aurelius was partly responsible for that.

FORGIVE THE ERRORS OF OTHERS

And what is it you will resent? Human wickedness? Recall the conclusion that rational creatures are born for each other's sake, that tolerance is a part of justice, that wrongdoing is not deliberate.[62]

Meditations – Marcus Aurelius, Book IV

It is sometimes very hard to forgive people for wrongs done to us, particularly if we feel we have been unjustly treated or betrayed in some way. A trust has been broken, maybe, and we feel let down, hurt and angry. The Stoics' view of forgiveness is entwined with their response to criticism or insults: we only remain angry and resentful if we choose to remain so. We can't go back in time and change what has occurred, but we can choose how to respond moving forward.

In the *Enchiridion*, Epictetus advises that if we reframe our thoughts and make them bereft of negative judgements we are often better able to see things as they are. (This Stoic practice is discussed

---

62 Marcus Aurelius, *Meditations*, p24

further in Chapter Four). He particularly stresses that we should not leap to judgements which may be inaccurate or damaging: 'Someone bathes in haste; don't say he bathes badly, but in haste. Someone drinks a lot of wine; don't say he drinks badly, but a lot. Until you know their reasons, how do you know that their actions are vicious?'[63]

Let's try it out by rephrasing the following sentence:

A. He or she has completely messed up again and ruined it for everyone.

B. He or she may have made a mistake which appears to have had an impact on some people.

Now let's analyse the language components of sentence A:

63 Epictetus, *Discourses*, p241

* He or she has <u>completely</u> messed up

<u>Completely</u> is an ungradable adverb. It cannot be modified: nothing can be 'a bit' completely or 'very' completely. So it has an unmistakable meaning. In sentence A, has he or she really <u>completely</u> messed up? Is nothing at all salvageable from the situation? That seems highly unlikely. After all, any apology, show of contrition or acceptance of responsibility represents a reparation.

* messed up <u>again</u>

The fact that he or she has made mistakes, or rather is judged to have made mistakes in the past, is irrelevant to the present situation – we can only control the present.

* and <u>ruined</u> it

'Ruined' seems somewhat harsh and definite – surely there is something that can be achieved to ameliorate the situation?

* for <u>everyone</u>

Again, this needs more than a little qualification – it is somewhat arrogant to speak on behalf of 'everyone'; maybe some people do not feel the same way?'

If you read the sentence back now it is easy to identify the anger in the judgements and the hyperbole in the expression, which is dripping in negativity.

Now let's break down sentence B in the same way and pose some questions:

* He or she <u>may have made</u> a mistake

Do we know for sure they made a mistake? Have they taken responsibility or are they being blamed? If it was a mistake, was that accidental or deliberate?

* which <u>appears to have had an impact</u> on some people

Do we know how other people have been impacted? Have they expressed any sense of hurt or disappointment?

By stripping the comments of their negative judgements we enter into a process of de-catastrophizing the situation, adopting the process of 'laying bare' that was discussed in connection with the discipline of judgement in Chapter Four. And through asking the right questions we are able to begin to close the gap between the perceived injury and a path towards resolution. As Marcus Aurelius writes:

'When someone does you wrong, you should consider immediately what judgement of good or evil led him to wrong you? When you see this, you will pity him, and not feel surprise or anger.'[64]

US rapper Lupe Fiasco is a follower of Stoicism and mentions Marcus Aurelius in one of his raps: 'Emperor is his alias, but not Marcus Aurelius'. He also recommended to his 2 million followers on twitter that they read *Meditations*, 'so we can all start on the same page'.

Evil is again meant in the Stoic sense of bad judgements, motivational forces and emotions, and good is meant to be the exercise of virtue.

In general, most human errors are understandable since they may have been choices made in bad faith. If they are followed by sincere contrition, they should be accepted with good grace. From a Stoic perspective people are only clouded by evil because they are ignorant

---

64 Marcus Aurelius, *Meditations*, p62

of the truth and have lost their ability to apply reason and virtue. By forgiving their errors we not only exercise our own sound judgement but we also provide them with a pathway to atonement and their own progress and self-development. In short, it's a win–win situation.

We cannot control the past. Put simply, what's done is done and cannot be undone. On occasion, no good will come by dwelling on things in the past, so, as the saying goes, it is wiser to let sleeping dogs lie. It is more important to let go and move on. Also, forgiveness is not the only aspect of the process. If there is still good that can be done, a positive outcome to be achieved moving forward, then the issue belongs in the present. If, however, that moment when a meaningful consequence can be realized has expired, then the issue should be confined to the past. In the end, as Marcus Aurelius observed '[People] are born for the sake of each other. So either teach or tolerate.'[65]

---

65   Ibid., p82

One of the main tutors to the young Marcus Aurelius was the Stoic philosopher Junius Rusticus. Marcus mentions Rusticus several times in *Meditations*, citing him as a major influence on his intellectual development. Rusticus was also the judge at the trial of Justin Martyr, an early Christian sentenced to death for his beliefs and the source of the word martyr.

Among the other misfortunes of humanity is this, that men's intellects are confused, and they not only cannot help going wrong, but love to go wrong. To avoid being angry with individuals, you must pardon the whole mass, you must grant forgiveness to the entire human race. If you are angry with young and old men because they do wrong, you will be angry with infants also, for they soon will do wrong.[66]

---

66 Seneca, 'On Anger', Book I, Chapter X

The Discipline of Emotions

This chapter has been emotional, or rather, has been about how we can discipline our emotions and direct our emotional impulses towards positive responses and outcomes. We have seen how negative thoughts provoke negative outcomes and discussed the vital need to find time to check our impulses that are provoked by the 'impressions' we receive.

We have also seen the negative energy that is produced through anger and the choice between using our resources of resilience, our courage in the face of adversity, or relinquishing control of a situation through fury or fear. And finally we have discussed the virtue of forgiving the error of others and learned how to rephrase or strip bare negative language in thoughts or utterances, and analyse them as a process of reparation of perceived injury or damage. The Stoics placed great value on emotional responses, not because they saw emotions as something to suppress, but because they saw emotions as something that needed to be exercised with discipline. The Greek Stoic Chrysippus said that the power of emotional pull is analogous to running too fast down a hill. The momentum builds and builds until it is impossible to suddenly stop without falling over. But as we have seen, we all have the tools to channel our emotions in constructive and not destructive ways.

Chapter Six

Understanding Nature

Always remember these things: what the nature of the Whole is, what my own nature is, the relation of this nature to that, what kind of part it is of what kind of Whole; and that there is no one who can prevent you keeping all that you say and do in accordance with the nature of which you are a part.[67]

Meditations – Marcus Aurelius, Book II

---

67 Marcus Aurelius, *Meditations*, p12

The Stoic philosophers put great stock in the power of nature and in fact use the term nature in several different contexts. Today we think of nature as the great outdoors – animals and plants and landscapes, areas relatively untouched by the more disruptive aspects of human society – and to some extent the Stoics also use the word nature in this way. But they also use the term nature in relation to what Marcus Aurelius describes as '*the Whole*'. By this they mean a godlike power that pervades every living thing and all of the universe, which they believe is connected as one sprawling organism and life force. It is this second, all-encompassing concept of the natural 'Whole' of existence that the Stoics refer to when they talk of 'living in accordance with nature'. That is to say, the most natural way to live is the most virtuous and thriving way, to be happy and achieve *eudaimonia*.

It is a curious fallacy of the human race that at some point we began to regard ourselves as somehow separated from nature. We developed civilizations that we believed could transcend, tame and control the natural world for our own ends. The folly of this way of thinking has certainly come back to haunt humankind with the current eco and climate change crises as nature has thrown everything it can back at us, with floods, draughts, wildfires and catastrophic storms now common occurrences. So there is something appealing about the Stoics' approach to nature, that we are part of it and to reach our full potential we must embrace and accept our place in the natural order of the universe and as part of 'the Whole'.

In this chapter we shall examine in closer detail the Stoic view of nature and 'the Whole', including how we should see ourselves in relation to the universe, accept the ever changing 'nature' of things, and accept the workings of fate compared to our expectations.

CONSIDER THE VIEW FROM ABOVE

Think of the whole of existence, of which you are the tiniest part; think of the whole of time, in which you have been assigned a brief and fleeting moment; think of destiny – what fraction of that are you?[68]

Meditations – Marcus Aurelius, Book IV

Marcus Aurelius devoted a great deal of time to meditating on his place in the wider scheme of things. By most measures, he was a great man, the last of Machiavelli's 'Five Good Emperors' (see Chapter Two). He was a shrewd military general, a clever diplomat and a skilful politician and, most importantly from our point of view, a wise and enquiring philosopher. What is interesting is the contempt he has for the idea of fame and legacy – the 'great man of history' syndrome that has consumed despots and dictators throughout time, often precipitating their downfall. Despite his fame, popularity and achievements, Marcus Aurelius comes across through his *Meditations* as a remarkably

---

68 Ibid., p42

humble man. He constantly chides and chastises the desire for fame, pointing out not only how damaging such a desire is to the soul, but also ultimately how futile it is.

One of Marcus' regular meditations is to try and consider the view from above, to step outside of ourselves. A step-by-step meditation practice to help with that is described in the Epilogue – but for now let's examine what Marcus Aurelius means by the 'view from above'.

Epictetus never wrote any of his teachings down but they survive due to the transcriptions from the notes of one his pupils Arrian who put together the different books of the *Discourses* and the *Enchiridion*. In addition to preserving the teachings of Epictetus, Arrian was also a renowned historian who wrote an important biography of Alexander the Great.

In the quote from Book IV of *Meditations* that prefaces this section, we are invited to consider 'the whole of existence'. It is quite a mind-blowing prospect to try to imagine the whole of existence, every particle of everything all around us. Then Marcus invites us to think of 'the whole of time', stretching back 13.8 billion years when the universe began and forward to infinity (my father, who was a physicist, would argue that as finite beings we are incapable of contemplating the infinite, but I'll return to that point later). The vastness of everything overwhelms us; we are but a tiny part of the Whole, apportioned only a tiny amount of time – 'a brief and fleeting moment' – with no influence upon the flow of destiny.

It could be argued that it may not be wise to spend time considering how insignificant our lives are, if ultimately they have no tangible purpose in the overall scheme of things. But if we look at it another way, the 'view from above' perspective can be a powerful spiritual tool to help us appreciate what we do have in our lives and in the world, and what actually matters.

In a speech at Cornell University, New York in 1994, Professor Carl Sagan, a NASA scientist, spoke about the contemplation of planet Earth from space, the ultimate 'view from above'. Sagan invited his audience to look at an image of the Earth taken from a Voyager spacecraft, and in a manner that echoed Marcus Aurelius, asked the audience to think of all human life and history which has taken place on 'the pale blue spot' that is planet Earth – all human triumphs and disasters, wars and human conflicts, human creations and endeavours, ideologies and religions – and consider their insignificance in relation to the vastness of the cosmos.

Sagan ended his speech by arguing that although 'our posturings, our imagined self-importance, the delusion that we have some privileged position in the Universe, are challenged by this point of pale light',[69] by viewing from above we are able to see how life on earth – the Whole, is to be valued. He stressed that we need to take responsibility for our part in it: 'There is perhaps no better demonstration of the folly of human conceits than this distant image of our tiny world. To me, it underscores our responsibility to deal more

69   Sagan, Carl, *Pale Blue Dot: A Vision of the Human Future in Space*, Ballantine Books Inc, New York, 1997, p382

kindly with one another, and to preserve and cherish the pale blue dot.'[70]

Sagan said that the view of our world from space provides an insight into our place in the infinite universe, and our fragile insignificance should be all the more treasured because of this.

NOTHING LASTS FOREVER

Reflect often on the speed with which all things in being, or coming into being, are carried past and swept away. Existence is like a river in ceaseless flow, its actions a constant succession of change.[71]

Meditations – Marcus Aurelius, Book IV

Another key component of the Stoic view of nature and the Whole is the impermanence of things. In nature things are always changing: plants and animals come into being, live and grow, wither and die. Marcus Aurelius

---

70 Ibid., p382

71 Marcus Aurelius, *Meditations*, p42

uses the metaphor of a river for existence in 'ceaseless flow', carrying things away from us and bringing new things before us.

People are fearful of change, anxious about what the future may look like or frightened of losing what they have. For the Stoics, as change in nature is inevitable and unavoidable, so too is change in our lives. Okay, so some people may live by a routine, do the same job for forty years, be partnered with the same person, go on holiday to the same place and probably feel that their life doesn't change, but it does. Just because the structure of their life appears on the surface to have remained static, the world and the people around them has changed and moved on.

Marcus Aurelius goes on to invite us to 'reflect too on the yawning gulf of past and future time, in which all things vanish'.[72] So what is in existence now won't be in the future, and what existed in the past will

72 Ibid., p42

eventually be forgotten. He then expands this point by chiding people for wasting time in the present in mental strife over things they cannot control, namely the inexorable passing of time: 'So all this must be folly for anyone to be puffed with ambition, racked in struggle, or indignant at his lot – as if this was anything lasting.'[73]

In Book V of *Meditations* Marcus Aurelius counsels against viewing change as something that is always for the best: 'Change: nothing inherently bad in the process, nothing inherently good in the result.'[74] Marcus is not suggesting that nothing positive can ever occur through change, just that the process of change itself is indifferent to measures of good or bad (it is a matter for our judgements to decide if a change is positive or negative). Furthermore we shouldn't fear change just because we are attached

---

73 Ibid., p42

74 Ibid., p31

to a certain set of circumstances or familiar with a situation. The key point is that if you accept that change is inevitable and things do not last forever, it's healthier to consent that change will occur and learn to adapt. It is certainly unhealthy to become stuck in your ways and aggrieved at or resentful of the inevitable changes.

Epictetus in the *Enchiridion* sets out a Stoic practice to help us deal with changes that may be disconcerting or upsetting, or that we may fear. His idea involves accepting the impermanence of things and people: 'In the case of things that delight you, or to which you have become attached remind yourself of what they are.'[75] Epictetus then suggests starting with a favourite object of little value, like an ornate piece of china, and to repeat to yourself, 'I like that china', but then imagine it smashed into pieces. His theory is that should fate occur and the ornament does get smashed, you will have already prepared for its loss.

This Stoic practice is known as *Premeditatio malorum* ('premeditation of evils') – a form of negative visualization which we will explore in Part Three. Epictetus then suggests: 'When giving your wife or child a kiss, repeat to yourself "I am kissing a mortal", then you won't be so distraught if they are

---

75 Epictetus, *Discourses*, p222

taken from you.'[76] Okay, it is something of a stretch of credulity to think that the accidental smashing of a favourite piece of china is in any sense comparable to the loss of a child or loved one. The point is that we should value what we have in the moment and be grateful for our good fortune to have things and people around us that give us pleasure and make us happy. We should be mindful not to take these things for granted as, sadly, we will not always have them – nothing lasts forever.

NATURE'S ORDER AND 'US'

Reflect on how separate events, both bodily and mental, are taking place in each of us in the same fragment of time: and then you will not be surprised if many more events, indeed all that comes to pass, subsist together in the one and the whole, which we call the universe.[77]

Meditations – Marcus Aurelius, Book VI

---

76   Ibid., p222

77   Marcus Aurelius, *Meditations*, p51

The founder of Stoicism, Zeno of Citium, first developed the concept that our lives should have a 'smooth flow' (think of Marcus Aurelius' river of existence), but it was his protégé and student, Cleanthes, who expanded the notion and suggested that all we do should be done in agreement or accordance 'with nature'.

As we have noted, nature was a word that the Stoics used in quite specific ways. It meant both nature as we understand it – the natural world in opposition to cities and manufactured things – but moreover they saw it as a 'Whole', an entire material universe which functions according to reason and connects to humans as part of the natural order of things, since we are at base animals, even if we are rational and social ones.

Zeno used the term *kathēkon* ('appropriate behaviour') to describe actions that are 'based in virtue and are carried out in accordance with our duty to the natural order'.[78] The concept became expanded, so that duty was seen as a central obligation to behave appropriately in our roles in domestic life and wider society. Zeno challenged his students to go on a spiritual and mental journey to a place where every action they considered was in harmonious accord with each man's guiding spirit and the will of the one who governs the universe.[79]

If the Stoics had a god, it would be nature, the universe and an all-encompassing power of which we too are a part. We share the divine spark in the form of *daimon*, or spirit guide (see Chapter Three), which belongs to the universal nature of all things, the Whole that Marcus Aurelius refers to over and over again. Those who live by keeping the individual and universal natures in harmony with each other achieve *eudaimonia* and are happy, and those who fail in this endeavour, for whatever reason, are unhappy.

---

78   Diogenes Laërtius, *Lives of Eminent Philosophers*, p305
79   Ibid., p305

For the Stoics the disconnection of these two natures is a root source of human misery and is not how we are meant to live. The solution is to apply wisdom (reason) in the course of everything we do and this requires devoting ourselves to Stoic practices, to trying to be the best version of ourselves because that is our position in nature's order. Marcus Aurelius summed this idea up perfectly when he wrote: 'For a rational being, to act in accordance with nature is also to act in accordance with reason.'[80]

---

80   Marcus Aurelius, *Meditations*, p60

From Nietzsche to Eternity

Although they never coined the phrase *Amor fati* ('love of fate') in their writings, all of the Stoics advocated accepting whatever fate befalls us with gratitude and good grace. The first person to actually use the term *Amor fati* explicitly was the German philosopher Friedrich Nietzsche (1844–1900) in a section of his autobiographical writings *Ecce Homo* - somewhat immodestly subtitled 'Why I Am So Clever'. In it he wrote: 'My formula for greatness in a human being is *amor fati*: that one wants nothing to be different, not forward, not backward, not in all eternity. Not merely bear what is necessary, still less conceal it – all idealism is mendacity in the face of what is necessary – but love it.'[81]

Amor fati appealed to Nietzsche due to his belief in what he termed 'eternal recurrence', a philosophical concept that time is trapped in an eternal loop and that the same events will repeat themselves over and over for all eternity. Hence, we cannot escape fate, so we may as well embrace it, or in the words of Marcus Aurelius: 'Love only what falls your way and is fated for you. What could suit you more than that?'

---

81 Nietzsche, Friedrich *Ecce Homo* in *Basic Writings of Nietzsche*, trans. Kaufmann, Walter (1908), Random House, New York, 2001, p.714.

ACCEPT THE FICKLENESS OF FATE AND FALSE EXPECTATIONS

Don't hope that events will turn out the way you want, welcome events in whichever way they happen: this is the path to peace.[82]

Enchiridion – Epictetus, Chapter 8

For Epictetus, in order for our life to flow well, we need to develop what Stoics refer to as 'the art of acquiescence', in short, letting go and moving on by accepting that 'whatever will be, will be'. This mindset applies both to past events and to future possibilities, and is an important factor in applying discipline both to our judgements and our emotions.

---

82   Epictetus, *Discourses*, p224

We have all suffered disappointments in our lives, things that have not turned out the way that we expected, and therein lies the folly of expectation.

In his *Consolation to Helvia,* one of the letters of condolences he wrote to family and friends while in exile on the island of Corsica, Seneca writes: 'No man loses anything by the frowns of Fortune unless he has been deceived by her smiles,'[83] which is a beautifully poetic way of saying we have been deluded into an expectation of what we wanted to happen rather than considering and preparing ourselves for all eventualities.

Seneca then goes on to describe a particular type of person, who in modern terms may be described as 'entitled' in their outlook: 'those who have enjoyed her bounty as though it were their own heritage forever, and who have chosen to take precedence of others because of it, lie in abject sorrow when her unreal and fleeting delights forsake their empty childish minds ...' People who take for granted their wealth, prestige and power, believing them to be their birthright and using them to exert their influence, are crushed when these things are suddenly taken away from them.

Some historical context can be applied to these elegant lines of Seneca. He had just suffered the indignity of having his power and influence stripped

---

83   Seneca, *Minor Dialogues*, pp.320–52

from him, so was only too aware of the fickleness of fate. Yet he seems sanguine about his misfortune. Seneca goes on to describe how the man who has not been 'puffed up by success, does not collapse after failure: for even in the midst of prosperity he has experimented upon his powers of enduring adversity'.[84]

It is unclear if Seneca is describing himself in these passages, possibly to reassure his mother that he is in acceptance of his misfortune and isn't about to take the Roman way out of getting into a hot bath then slashing his wrists. Beyond his personal circumstances, however, Seneca is making a broader point about resilience and the art of acquiescence. Firstly, we should mentally prepare ourselves for situations that may not turn out the way we want, and beware of inflating our expectations, or as Seneca describes, bloating our sense of entitlement. Secondly, if and

---

84   Ibid.

when things don't go our way, we need to accept them as they are and move forward with whatever situation we find ourselves in.

When my father was succumbing to Alzheimer's disease it was obviously a very difficult time for the family. It seemed particularly unfair and cruel for such a kind, gentle, thoughtful and intellectual man to suffer degenerative brain disease. It would have been easy for us as a family to get angry and resentful and think 'What have we done to deserve this?' However, as Marcus Aurelius observed when discussing anger, we should not let circumstances beyond our control provoke us, for the circumstances in themselves have no feelings for us; fate is dispassionate and indiscriminate, it simply doesn't care. So as a family we adopted a phrase which we often repeated to each other: 'It is what it is'. All we could do was deal with the situation in front of us.

The same is also true of past events. We have all experienced regrets about past situations, as well as opportunities missed or wasted. There is little point dwelling upon past events, certainly not becoming anguished about them: it is much easier to move on. I often bring to mind the opening lines of a song by the rock band Butthole Surfers on the subject of past disappointments in that 'it's better to regret something you have done, than to regret something you haven't done'.[85] If you did do something you regret, you can accept your mistake and can vow not to make the same error of judgement in the future.

Some Stoics, such as Epictetus, suggest an expansion of the art of acquiescence, whereby we not only accept the sometimes cruel and fickle trappings of fate but actually positively welcome them: 'It is easy to praise providence for everything that happens in the world provided you have the ability to see individual events

85 'Sweat Loaf' by Butthole Surfers, from the album *Locust Abortion Technician*, Side A, track 1, Touch And Go Records, 1987

in the context of the Whole and a sense of gratitude.'[86] This process is referred to by modern Stoics as *Amor fati* (see 'From Nietzsche to Eternity'), which translates as 'love of fate', and is a mental state of not only showing gratitude for whatever happens to you but also seeing it as necessary. This approach ties in to some degree with seeing adversity as a positive challenge and an opportunity for growth.

---

86 Epictetus, *Discourses*, p16

Understanding Nature

In this chapter we have looked in some detail at the Stoic view of nature as something all encompassing, something that we, albeit in a tiny way, are a part of and can benefit from understanding it and living in accord with it. Sometimes it helps to try to view ourselves and our world from a lofty perspective, as thinkers from Marcus Aurelius to Professor Carl Sagan have done. We have also discussed how nothing is permanent and that our lives and our world are subject to constant change. On occasion we may not like these changes as they could lead to outcomes that were unexpected or unfortunate, but we must resolve to take things as they are, for our world 'is what it is'.

Imagine you were now dead, or had not lived before this moment. Now view the rest of your life as a bonus, and live it as nature directs.[87]

Meditations - Marcus Aurelius, Book VII

87   Marcus Aurelius, *Meditations*, p56

Chapter Seven

Living With Ourselves and Others

Wherever there is a human being, there is an opportunity for kindness.[88]

Minor Dialogues – Seneca

---

88 Seneca, *Minor Dialogues*, pp.320–52

In this chapter we shall look at how the practice of Stoicism can be applied to the way we live and interact with others and the wider communities to which we belong. Thus far, we have concentrated on mastering skills of self-control and nurturing calmness, self-reflection and resilience. The question now is how these skills can be reconciled with our responsibilities to others as well as to ourselves. We shall examine the nature of kindness and gracious actions; discover how we can cope with the obstacles and challenges that society brings to bear upon us; discuss the value of speaking less and listening more; and finally contemplate the nature of death and dealing with grief.

In *Meditations*, Epictetus is mentioned several times, but Marcus Aurelius never mentions Seneca. It is known that Marcus Aurelius studied Seneca as a letter survives from his rhetoric tutor, Marcus Cornelius Fronto, advising him to stop reading Seneca's works. Fronto argues that Seneca's writing is all superficial flourishes with little substance and equivalent to searching through the sewers for silver coins.

Let's take as a stepping-off point the central Stoic concept of the cultivation of virtue and living a virtuous life. What value would the virtues of calmness, loyalty, empathy, understanding and kindness hold if they weren't practised in society?

'Man is by nature a social animal ... society is something that precedes the individual', wrote Aristotle, and this is a principle upheld by the Stoics. Understanding how to live within society and accepting the responsibility to do so with virtue and grace is mentioned again and again by the Stoics. 'A person cannot attain any good for themselves unless they contribute some service to the community,'[89] wrote Epictetus.

The Roman Stoic philosopher Musonius Rufus drew an analogy between human society and bees, stating that 'a bee is unable to live alone for it perishes in isolation'. A churlish counter would be to argue that it is possible for humans to live outside society – in solitary self-

89 Epictetus, *Discourses*, p222

sufficiency. Yet are such hermits really 'living'? Aristotle disagreed, arguing that 'Anyone who either cannot lead the common life or is so self-sufficient as not to need to, and therefore does not partake of society, is either a beast or a god.' Or as Marcus Aurelius elegantly stated, 'What brings no benefit to the hive, brings none to the bee.'[90]

The Stoics placed kindness at the centre of their list of core virtues. Seneca in particular placed great value on kindness as a character trait to be practised and nurtured. There are, however, differing views between the classical Stoic philosophers on the concept of the debt of gratitude. This relates to how we react to the giving and receiving of favours. In *Meditations*, Marcus Aurelius makes a distinction between three types of character in relation to acts of kindness. The first type bestows a kindness upon another and immediately demands one in return. The second bestows a kindness and although they may not immediately demand

---

90 Marcus Aurelius, *Meditations*, p57

recompense, they nonetheless regard the recipient as being in debt to them. The third, a true Stoic, asks for nothing in return for their favour, for the act in itself is reward enough: 'like the vine which has produced grapes and looks for nothing else once it has borne its own fruit'.[91]

Seneca, however, believed that when receiving a favour from another person the recipient did owe a debt of gratitude. He stated: 'He is ungrateful who denies that he has received a kindness, which has been bestowed upon him; he is ungrateful who conceals it; he is ungrateful who makes no return for it; most ungrateful of all is he who forgets it.'[92]

If we are to believe in the concept that the goodness inherent in the act itself is its own just rewards, why then should there be a requirement to settle the debt of gratitude? I think the key is how we respond to favours and kindnesses we receive from others, and not to take them for granted.

BE NO STRANGER TO KINDNESS

During the global Covid-19 pandemic lockdowns there were many examples of communities that had become disconnected through enforced isolation, nonetheless,

91 Ibid., p37

92 Seneca, *Minor Dialogues*, pp320–52

finding ways to pull together, protect the vulnerable, and help and care for one another. A friend of mine, Joe, took to doing the weekly grocery shopping for his elderly neighbour, Sylvie. Joe hadn't had much to do with his neighbour prior to the pandemic bar the most cursory of acknowledgements when passing in the street.

Joe discovered from another neighbour that Sylvie had recently undergone treatment for cancer and so was required under government guidelines to self-isolate as she was considered high risk given the weakness of her immune system. As Joe works in the bakery department of a large supermarket he offered to collect Sylvie's groceries. Once a week, Sylvie telephoned Joe her shopping list, he picked them up from his place of work, wiped them down with sanitizer and left them on her porch.

A small act of kindness for a neighbour during a national emergency, one of many such acts at the time, is hardly a big deal or qualifies Joe for sainthood. It is, however, what happened after lockdown restrictions were lifted that Joe's Stoicism was put to the test. Joe continued to do Sylvie's weekly shopping for about six months post-pandemic but then moved to a new house on the other side of town. When Joe suggested to Sylvie that he would no longer be able to do her shopping for practical reasons she became agitated and upset. Noticing that Sylvie had a smartphone, Joe suggested a solution. He downloaded the supermarket app onto her smartphone and showed her how to make online delivery orders.

This seemingly simple solution to the problem, however, instantly became the problem. Sylvie was not very tech-savvy to say the least, and proceeded to bombard Joe with panicked phone calls when left on her own to place her online order. The internet had gone down, the order hadn't turned up, she'd ordered twice/paid twice by mistake, someone had hacked her account, etc. Each trauma, major or minor, was followed by a plaintive plea for Joe to come round and help fix things.

Now Joe is a kind man, but his patience was being tested and nobody likes to feel their best intentions are being exploited. So, he stepped back from the situation and his growing feelings of frustration and irritation and asked himself the question: 'Why can't Sylvie do her own shopping?' He had shown her several times how to use the app and place an order; she had even done it herself in front of him and written down step-by-step instructions. Sylvie's health had improved considerably, and she was being advised by her doctor to exercise more, so she was physically capable of going to the supermarket by herself. The answer had nothing to do with Sylvie's ability to do shopping in person or online, and everything to do with her personal situation. Living alone, recovering from a long illness, forced to self-isolate for months on end, she'd possibly developed some form of agoraphobia, but most likely she was just very, very lonely and for a long time Joe had been her only contact with the outside world.

On coming to this realization, Joe suggested they return to the old system they used during the pandemic, whereby Sylvie telephoned through her shopping list and Joe collected and delivered it to her door. Joe and Sylvie have since become good friends and he stays for a chat and has tea and cake when he delivers her shopping. Sylvie has also attended church with Joe and he has encouraged her to get in contact with friends with whom she had lost touch. It's a small act of kindness, but such small acts can mean a great deal to people.

Acts of kindness for a Stoic are integral to living a virtuous life, and furthermore the example of Joe and Sylvie illustrates another Stoic view of kindness: sharing aspects of life with other people unequivocally and without condition or question. Seneca writes that 'No good thing is pleasant to possess without having friends to share it with,'[93] and moreover 'No one can live happily who has regard to himself alone and transforms everything into a question of his own utility; you must live for your neighbour, if you would live for yourself.'[94]

---

93 Seneca, *Letters from a Stoic*, pp96–7

94 Ibid., pp96–7

EVERY CHALLENGE IS AN OPPORTUNITY

The mind adapts and turns
round any obstacle to action to
serve its objective: a hindrance
to a given work is turned into a
furtherance. An obstacle in a given
path becomes an advance.

Meditations – Marcus Aurelius, Book V

This quote may seem familiar to you, assuming you have been paying attention, because we discussed it before in Chapter Five in relation to our choice between 'Courage and Calm' or 'Fear and Fury'. I am revisiting it here because I think it deserves closer analysis and because it is such an iconic part of Stoicism in general. What Marcus Aurelius is saying is that there is nothing that we cannot overcome and gain a positive outcome from if we apply due reason and view it in the following way. It's an old cliché that has been trotted out since time immemorial but basically it amounts to saying 'whatever doesn't kill you, makes you stronger'.

The key to grasping this and, more importantly, actively accepting the concept and adopting it as a mantra lies in understanding the first part of Marcus' quote: 'The mind adapts and turns round any obstacle to action to serve its objective ...' This is slightly misleading as it seems to suggest that this process happens involuntarily and instinctively. In some senses it does, for example, if you are driving through a forest and you come across a fallen tree blocking your path, instinctively your objective would be to find a way around the obstacle blocking your pathway. However, our minds don't always work this way when obstacles and adversities present themselves. We become lost in a fog of anxiety about how we should approach a problem, we suffer all sorts of fears, from fear of failure, to fear of doing something wrong that may be harmful to our future.

Nassim Nicholas Taleb, the prominent mathematician and writer, is an avid follower of Stoicism and he defines a Stoic as someone *'who transforms fear into prudence, pain into transformation, mistakes into initiation, and desire into undertaking'.*

Epictetus counsels us to let go of these fears with the following advice: 'For every challenge, remember the resources you have within you to cope. Provoked by desire you will discover the contrary power of self-restraint. Faced with pain you will discover the power of endurance. If you are insulted, you will discover patience.'[95]

Think of this mental process as akin to the law of physics where every action has an opposite and equal reaction that can cancel it out. (The Stoics, incidentally, regarded physics as one of the 'noble pursuits' of knowledge, and placed great emphasis on it, alongside philosophy.)

Let's take the example of serious illness. Many

---

95 Epictetus, *Discourses*, p225

people have concerns about their health, which often feeds in to anxieties around our own mortality (see 'Dealing with Grief and Death' later in this chapter). Say, for example, a person is facing a serious operation or a series of prolonged medical interventions and treatments. Firstly, it is impossible to predict the outcome, and to some degree the outcome may be determined by matters beyond your control – so let's apply some *Amor fati*, 'what will be will be'. Secondly, having accepted our possible fate, we can now relax and identify how we can gain positives from the adversity. For example, we can learn much more about our bodies than we previously understood. We could partake in meditations or healing therapies which would be beneficial to us and encourage healthy habits. We could use the time while convalescing to take stock of our lives, perhaps keep a journal of the whole experience, read books about positive thinking, or simply just read books. There are endless positive outcomes to be gained from a daunting and potentially overwhelming time of adversity. As Epictetus concludes: 'In time, you will grow to be confident that there is not a single impression that you will not have the moral means to tolerate.'[96]

---

96   Ibid., p225

SOME THINGS ARE BEST LEFT UNSAID

Let silence be your goal for the most part; say only what is necessary and be brief about it.[97]

Enchiridion – Epictetus, Chapter 33

Of the 'Big Three' Stoic philosophers, I find Epictetus the hardest to fathom at times. Some of his proclamations seem to be quite severe, particularly in the *Enchiridion* where occasionally they can be read as rather preacher-like. However, if we put his life in context, we perhaps have to cut him some slack. Epictetus was born into slavery, so was hard-wired to be reticent, to only speak when spoken to. The section quoted above continues with a list of things people shouldn't speak of including 'banalities like gladiators, horses, sports, food and drink. Commonplace stuff'. This seems a little akin to the old adage that there are certain things which shouldn't be discussed in British pubs, namely the firebrand subjects of politics, religion and football. Epictetus mentions sports as unworthy of discourse, but not the other two, however.

---

97   Ibid., p236

Here is a short thought experiment you can do next time you are in a group of people socializing. Remain silent as often as possible and listen and observe how the interactions play out. It is quite staggering how often people interject only to end up talking about themselves. I have tried this with some members of my family, whom I won't name (I'm sure they know who they are anyhow), and actually play a game of mental bingo – ticking off when certain subjects will get mentioned and brought up in conversation, regardless of their relevance. That said, I don't doubt that I am equally guilty of the same behaviour on occasion and am equally oblivious to the situation. There are, however, two points which I feel Epictetus doesn't address. Firstly, yes, talking too much, especially about yourself, isn't a particularly appealing character trait, however if we listen properly and intently we can get a broader understanding of a person. Secondly, silence should only be our goal because we want to listen or become better listeners, and we can't be better listeners if we are doing all the talking.

The title of this section is 'Some Things Are Best Left Unsaid'. How many times have we said something in the heat of the moment that has provoked discord or caused distress to others which we did not intend or perhaps were not even aware of? How can we stop doing that? We can't control how other people react to the things that we say, but we do have control over the words that we say.

One simple Stoic practice if we find ourselves suddenly provoked is to rehearse in our mind what we are going to say before we blurt it out. This is easier said than done if we find ourselves in conflict with somebody who has raised our emotions. Take a few deep breaths, in your mind say what you were going to say and evaluate what kind of response it is likely to receive. If that response is unlikely to be in any way positive, hit the delete button on your mental keyboard, for some things are better left unsaid.

DEALING WITH GRIEF AND DEATH

Consider each individual thing you do and ask yourself whether to lose it through death makes death itself any cause for fear.[98]

Meditations – Marcus Aurelius, Book X

The Stoics, perhaps all philosophers, had a curious relationship with death. We have discussed the inevitability of change and also the need to accept the fickleness of fate. If there is one thing we can be very sure of (along with taxes, as the saying goes) it is that we are going to die. Marcus Aurelius seems to be questioning why we are so preoccupied with death and moreover why that should stop us from doing anything in the here and now. In short, what do we have to lose if we do something? After all, when we are dead we are, quite literally, dead.

Marcus Aurelius, as we have discussed previously, totally rejected the idea of fame or historical legacy, something which was a preoccupation of many Roman emperors before him, and sadly after his passing, too.

---

98   Marcus Aurelius, *Meditations*, p101

In another section of *Meditations*, quite possibly written around the same time as the quote above, he describes fame, prominence and success as mere leaves on a tree that have grown, but will soon wither and die and be replaced. Marcus Aurelius then expands this metaphor for all things in the Universe: 'All things are short-lived – his is their common lot – but [we] pursue likes and dislikes as if all was fixed for eternity'.[99] Thus we come again to this idea of accepting and embracing change, even if that change is ultimately our own mortality.

Seneca's contribution to the Stoic view of death and grief is encapsulated in his *Consolations*, his letters written to friends and family who had suffered the loss of a loved one. The *Consolations* are an uncomfortable read at times, and there is a strong suspicion beyond the eloquent purple prose (I have only read various English translations, some of which embellish the

99   Ibid., p103

dramatist in Seneca's writing more than others) that there isn't an awful lot of compassion or empathy on display. The following passage is quite extraordinary in its heartlessness and comes from his 'Consolation to Marcia' (*De Consolatione ad Marciam*):

'... if fate can be overcome by tears, let us bring tears to bear upon it: let every day be passed in mourning, every night be spent in sorrow instead of sleep: let your breast be torn by your own hands, your very face attacked by them, and every kind of cruelty be practised by your grief, if it will profit you. But if the dead cannot be brought back to life, however much we may beat our breasts, if destiny remains fixed and immoveable forever, not to be changed by any sorrow, however great, and death does not loosen his hold of anything that he once has taken away, then let our futile grief be brought to an end.'[100]

It is a long passage, but it is worth the long quotation as it encapsulates the Stoic view of death on one hand, and on the other hand is staggeringly thoughtless. It can be paraphrased in modern parlance as 'for goodness sake stop with all this wailing and snivelling, it isn't going to change anything, your son has been dead for three years and frankly we are all getting a bit bored

---

100 Wikisource in Seneca, *Minor Dialogues: Together with the Dialogue 'On Clemency'*, trans. Stewart, Aubrey, George Bell and Sons, London, 1900

of your grief'. Who needs enemies when you can have friends like that?

Yet beyond our natural aversion to what the good Senator Seneca seems to be saying, it is hard not to agree with his principles. I lost my father recently. Although it was expected, it still hurts, but I console myself with the thought that my father, a scientist, pragmatist and natural Stoic, would not want me to grieve obsessively for him – for he would say the same as Seneca – 'What purpose is it serving? I'm still dead. Don't waste your time.' The people that we loved and have been lost to us live on in our minds.

I'll leave the last word on death to Emperor Marcus Aurelius, who suffered the deaths of several of his children, surely the greatest pain anyone can be expected to endure, and yet accepted that these things happen and we shouldn't fear them for 'Death is relief from reaction to the senses, from the puppet strings of impulse, from the analytical mind, and from service to the flesh.'[101]

101   Marcus Aurelius, *Meditations*, p51

Living With Ourselves and Others

In this chapter we have discussed the importance of kindness as a means of developing a virtuous character and concluded that a kind act itself is a just reward. We have revisited again the idea that obstacles and challenges put in front of us can be viewed not as hindrances but as opportunities for learning, growth and self-improvement. Listening and being a good listener are skills too often overlooked but conversely we must be aware of the implications of the things we say and try to mentally rehearse our responses, for some things are best left unsaid. Epictetus has counselled us not to waste time on banal conversations but sometimes small talk is good and a way of forging connections. Finally we have contemplated our own mortality and discussed how we can prepare ourselves for the inevitability of death, something which people approach in different ways, and yet acceptance of loss is part of the process of grieving and a step towards conquering our fears. The Stoics spoke often of living each day as if it is our last and this brings to mind Epictetus' mantra:

'We must make the best of what is in our powers and take the rest as nature gives it.'[102]

---

102 Epictetus, *Discourses*, p7

PART THREE

EACH DAY IN THE LIFE OF A PRACTISING STOIC

Ten Stoic exercises to practise every day

So we reach the final act of our survey of Stoic philosophy, but this is far from the end of the story. Stoicism is a practical philosophy, not a purely theoretical one. I have attempted, where possible, to offer some tips, exercises and everyday examples in relation to Stoic principles and ideas, but this has only just scratched the surface of what is possible.

To this end I have outlined ten simple Stoic exercises which can be practised every day. Some of them are Stoic adaptations of mental exercises similar to those that are used in some forms of counselling and cognitive behaviour therapies, and because they are simple and straightforward, they require no specialist knowledge or equipment other than an open and enquiring mind. Now is the time to take up the Stoic mantle, for as Marcus Aurelius wrote: 'No more roundabout discussion of what makes a good person. Be one!'[103]

---

103   Marcus Aurelius, *Meditations*, p99

1.

ENVISAGE THE DAY AHEAD

On waking in the morning, before doing anything else, make some time to contemplate the day ahead of you. This can be done when still lying in bed, or during a trip to the bathroom, while under the shower or sitting at the kitchen table over a cup of tea or coffee – the important thing is to find the space and time to do this reflection–projection exercise *before* your proper day begins. So do not check your phone for messages or switch on your laptop or flick on the TV – you must be completely free from any outside stimulus or distraction.

Now consider the day ahead of you. What are you going to be doing? Is your life fairly routine? If so, think through your day, step by step. What obstacles or issues are you likely or possibly going to encounter as you progress through your day? If such problems arise or such situations come to pass, how are you going to deal with them? Are they situations or problems that are within your control?

Once you have imagined the day, step by step, now consider the following: is everything you are going to do this day necessary? What if today was to be your last day in this world? How would you spend it then? What would you do differently? In one of his letters to his friend Lucilius, Seneca suggests this mental reflection: 'Every day should be regulated as if it were the one that brings up the rear, the one that rounds out and completes our lives.' So, if this day is 'rounding out' our life, what can we do according to our virtues? As an exercise, identify one or two Stoic virtues such as justice, wisdom, temperance or courage and think of a situation where you can apply it. Maybe stop and speak to the homeless person you see outside your train station and offer to buy them a hot drink. Compliment a work colleague on their appearance or mediate in a dispute to settle an argument, maybe vow to not become agitated or annoyed if your bus is delayed or someone jumps the queue. By anticipating problems, identifying

what our reactions would be and pledging to act according to our virtues and principles, we are ready and prepared for the day that we are treating as if it is our last:

Perfection of character is this: to live each day as if it were your last, without frenzy, without apathy, without pretence.[104]

---

104   Ibid., p69

2.

PREMEDITATIO MALORUM: NEGATIVE VISUALIZATION

One of the aspects of the morning meditation on the day ahead of us is a process called negative visualization. In this we anticipate problems and obstacles or things that could go wrong during the day ahead. Seneca used the term *premeditatio malorum*, which roughly translates from Latin as 'premeditation of evils', and mentions it in a letter to Lucilius. In this letter, Seneca describes how his friend Liberalis was completely devastated by a fire in his home city of Lyon in what was Roman-occupied Gaul. Seneca reports that the fire completely razed the city to the ground and that even earthquakes do not wreak such total destruction.

Seneca goes on to ruminate that the human impact was not so much that fires occur (the Great Fire of Rome under Nero's reign happened the previous year in AD 64) but that it was so unforeseen and ferocious: 'What is quite unlooked for is more crushing in its effect, and unexpectedness adds to the weight of the disaster.'[105] To mitigate the impact, Seneca suggests that: 'We should project our thoughts ahead of us at every turn and have in mind every possible eventuality instead of only the usual course of events.'[106]

As part of the morning anticipation of the day's events, the negative visualization could include such things as a presentation at work going wrong, a job interview not going to plan, being delayed by something, becoming involved in an accident, or losing our wallet or door keys. In the morning *Premeditatio malorum* we project ourselves as dealing calmly with what is in our control and anticipate our responses to problems, but the process can be expanded to larger life choices and events. These could be issues such as financial worries, health concerns, the loss of a loved one or problems in our personal relationships.

---

105   Seneca, *Letters from a Stoic*, p178

106   Ibid., p178

By way of illustration, let's examine anticipating possible conflicts in a personal relationship.

A. *First find a quiet place where you can calm your mind without distractions. Take a series of deep breaths and close your eyes.*

B. *Think about your relationship and what triggers arguments and disagreements. Are the differences insurmountable?*

C. *Now try to 'walk in their shoes'. Look at the conflict from their situation. Think about how you respond to them. Could you respond in a more positive manner, displaying empathy and consideration?*

D. *Finally, think of actions you can take to avoid the conflicts arising in the first place.*

It is worth striking a note of caution here, the point of *Premeditatio malorum* is to foster resilience and prepare for possible obstacles. It is not to make ourselves unnecessarily anxious or depressed. It is also important not to dwell on negative outcomes for an extended period of time. Remember, for Stoics things aren't bad in themselves, it is only that we perceive them as being bad: most situations are neutral impressions until we react and form our judgements of them. To dwell over and over on the same negative outcomes risks strengthening those negative impressions on our mind. So once we have gone through the process of negative visualization, reward ourselves with the thought that these bad things haven't happened yet and we are prepared for them if they should occur.

3.

THE VIEW FROM ABOVE

In Chapter Six we discussed the Stoic practice of trying to see the world from above. Marcus Aurelius, a man who suffered countless crises, both personally and as emperor of Rome, often practised this meditation:

Take a view from above – look at the thousands of human ceremonies, every sort of voyage in storm or calm, the range of creation, combination and extinction.[107]

In order to follow Marcus' practice, take these steps:

A. *Go to your quiet place of meditation, although actually this exercise can work well outside in nature, in a park or on a beach,*

---

107   Marcus Aurelius, *Meditations*, p89

but preferably on an empty beach or in a park at a time when few people are around.

B. *Close your eyes and breathe deeply until you feel your mind clearing of thoughts.*

C. *As thoughts drift in and out of your mind, don't engage with them but try to separate yourself from them, as if you are outside of your mind looking in. Imagine you are looking into your mind through a window.*

D. *You should now begin to detach your mind from your body. Try to envisage your spirit floating out and rising above your physical body.*

E. *Allow yourself to gradually float higher and higher so that you are looking down on your body, the park or beach, the town or city, the country, the continent, the globe ... Think in terms of slowly zooming out from a point in Google Maps.*

F. *As you look down on the earth the way astronauts in the International Space Station do, follow the advice of Marcus Aurelius: 'consider the range of creation, combination and extinction'. Think of the millions of years of life on earth, not just human life, but plant life, animal life, organisms in the oceans, rivers, jungles, and swamps. In this respect the part we play is miniscule and insignificant in the timeline of existence, and so are our worries and our troubles.*

G. *When you are feeling freed from the anxieties that were gripping you, start a slow descent back down to earth, to your continent, your country, your town, your park bench or beach and your mortal body waiting to reconnect with you.*

It is to be hoped that by doing the meditation you are able to adopt a different perspective on your own life, what is important to you, and what causes you to feel pain and anxiety. Our place within the universe is part of a scheme encompassing and connecting all things, and Marcus Aurelius recognized the power of this contemplation when he wrote:

Observe the movement of the stars as if you were running their courses with them, and let your mind constantly dwell on the changes of the elements into each other. Such imaginings wash away the filth of life on the ground.[108]

Meditations – Marcus Aurelius, Book VII

108   Ibid., p65

4.

DO ONE PIECE OF LIFE LAUNDRY A DAY

Epictetus, in the second book of his *Discourses*, devotes a considerable amount of thought to our daily habits, particularly our most unappealing faults and foibles: 'Every habit and faculty is strengthened by the corresponding act – walking makes you walk better, running makes you a better runner.'[109] This is sound advice: practise anything for twenty to thirty minutes a day and you can master it. Okay, you may never be able to play the guitar like Jimi Hendrix or B. B. King, but you will learn the basics of how to play the instrument if you make a habit of practising it.

But what of bad habits? Epictetus, in a section titled 'On Inconsistency', has concerns that we

---

109 Epictetus, *Discourses*, p126

do not fully accept some of our faults: 'People are ready to acknowledge some of their faults but will admit to others only with reluctance. No one, at any rate, will admit to being stupid … In general, where people are led to acknowledge a fault it is because they imagine there is something involuntary about it.'[110] This line of reasoning is a flimsy excuse at best, and bad faith and a failure of reasoning at worst.

One exercise Stoics can do, though, is to make a list of what they consider to be their most unappealing habits or inconsistencies. These can be minor, seemingly trivial things, like being slow at returning people's calls when they leave a message, not putting the recycling out, or not taking time to stop and have a chat with your neighbours when you meet them in the street, instead hurrying on past pretending to be busy when you weren't actually in any hurry at all.

Or the list could contain more serious 'bad habits', such as always being late for appointments or meeting friends. The list could include paying

---

110   Ibid., p133

bills late because you 'haven't got round to it'; neglecting to keep in touch with family and old friends; or borrowing things and not to return them in the state in which you received them. In short, not showing respect and courtesy to other people because you are too wrapped up in your own life to consider someone else.

These unappealing habits can be easily broken once they have been identified, so during the morning meditation identify one piece of this sort of 'life laundry' to address that day. It could be paying a bill you have left outstanding, it could be fixing a new washer on a leaking tap in the bathroom, it could be replying to an email from an old friend. It doesn't have to be a major action, but should be something that you have been putting off, or got into the habit of ignoring. One method for dealing with habits which we have let become part of us is to deliberately set about creating a contrary habit. So, if you are always late, put your watch forward ten minutes and be deliberately early.

5.

HAVE SOME TIME OUT – TURN OFF THE NOISE

If you want to make progress, put up with being perceived as ignorant or naïve in worldly matters, don't aspire to a reputation for sagacity.[111]

Enchiridion – Epictetus, Chapter 13

In the modern age of 24/7 news it's often difficult to escape what is happening in the world. Our smartphones buzz with notifications of something deemed immediately newsworthy, as if our lives

---

111 Ibid., p226

would be impoverished if we didn't know what was happening somewhere, somehow, right here, or there or everywhere, right now, this very minute.

The speed in which information is processed and dispersed in modern life is bewildering, confusing and often a cause in itself of anxiety. But how much of this information is actually relevant to our everyday life?

This is not to say we should bury our heads in the ground and pretend all of the bad things in the world aren't really happening. Nor should we take the position that even if bad things are happening there isn't much we can do about it. Taking time out is about maintaining a balance, developing internal mental filters to stop our brains from reaching information overload. Just as sports teams use 'time-outs' to strategically stop the clock, regroup and reset their goals, we should, from time to time, do exactly the same in our lives.

In one slightly curious section of his *Discourses*, Epictetus makes an argument for the circumstances and reasons why somebody should or shouldn't read a book:

A book is external, just like office or public

honours – why do you want to read anyway – for the sake of amusement or mere erudition? Those are poor, fatuous pretexts. Reading should serve the goal of attaining peace; if it doesn't make you peaceful, what good is it?[112]

I'm not sure I entirely agree with Epictetus regarding the value of reading in relation to erudition. No doubt Epictetus would concur that nobody likes a smart alec, and showing off one's intelligence for the sake of ego or to gain influence is certainly not a Stoic practice. But reading for learning and self-improvement is surely laudable and to be commended? And what of erudition? To communicate our thoughts and feelings

---

112   Ibid., p198

clearly and elegantly without ambiguity is also an admirable quality to nurture – is that not part of the process of philosophy? What I take Epictetus to mean, if we focus on the second part of his aphorism, is that reading should encourage 'peace of mind' through learning, not anxiety and discord through reading something for reasons we are not even capable of articulating to ourselves.

So, for at least part of the day, or if we are feeling really adventurous, try a whole twenty-four hours, take a 'time-out' from news websites and applications, radio bulletins and podcasts, don't turn on the TV or read a newspaper, resist the tempting allure of the 'click bait' pop-ups on the laptop, and spend some time with your own thoughts. This is especially something which should be done at the end of the day (see number 10).

6.

DISCARD SOMETHING YOU DON'T NEED

Another inevitable by-product of consumer capitalism and the digital age is the amount of 'stuff' we accumulate. This is particularly true of devices such as smartphones and tablets (I have boxes full of obsolete chargers and leads), but it is also true in a more general sense – we are bombarded with advertising which is designed to make us feel we need this 'stuff', that this 'stuff' will enrich our lives. We are enslaved by the technology we have created. But do we really need it all?

Two thousand years ago, Seneca noted the human appetite for acquiring 'stuff' in a letter to his friend Lucilius:

'Therefore, with regard to the objects which we pursue, and for which we strive with great effort, we should note this truth; either there is nothing desirable in them, or the undesirable is preponderant. Some objects are superfluous; others are not worth the price we pay for them. But we do not see this clearly, and we regard things as free gifts when they really cost us very dear.'[113]

Seneca is pointing to the grip that these objects have upon us, the amount of time we apportion to using them and the emotional energy expended upon them when they break down. Things seem to be so much worse today – the Wi-Fi is out, or the battery is dying, or we drop our phone or lose it. Then there are the digital subscriptions, the endless free trials of streaming

---

113   Seneca, *Moral Epistles to Lucilius*, Letter 42

services, software platforms and cloud space (I wonder what Seneca would have made of free trial offers?) that really cost us dear because we forget about them and don't cancel them in time. And all the time we suffer the incessant ping of notifications and reminders to update to the latest versions of everything.

We also have other physical objects cluttering up our lives that we don't need: that jacket you bought on a whim but have never worn; a holiday souvenir which seemed like a good purchase at the time but you can no longer remember why you bought it; a gaudy Christmas jumper or novelty T-shirt someone bought you as a joke present. We can get rid of all this stuff because, as Seneca says, 'some objects are superfluous'.

So alongside taking some time out, before you do so, discard something you don't need or use. In digital terms this can be unsubscribing from an email newsletter you rarely read and just clogs up your email inbox, or deleting an app you never use. In physical terms, take a bag of clothes you never wear to the charity shop or give something away to someone who may appreciate it or use it. Once you have discarded the thing you have identified as unnecessary, consider for a moment or two the example of the forefather of Stoicism, the Cynic philosopher Crates of Thebes, who gave away all of his wealth and possessions to live among the poor of Athens and enjoyed a happy and contented life. By ridding ourselves of things we don't need we create more space to think freely, unencumbered by external distractions.

7.

FOSTER PHILANTHROPY

For anyone who receives a benefit more gladly than he repays it is mistaken. By as much as he who pays is more light-hearted than he who borrows, by so much ought he to be more joyful who unburdens himself of the greatest debt – a benefit received – than he who incurs the greatest obligations.[114]

Moral Epistles to Lucilius – Seneca, Letter 81

The Stoics say that philanthropy does not mean that we have to follow Crates' example by giving

---

114   Seneca, *Moral Epistles to Lucilius*, Letter 13 'On Groundless Fear'

away all our worldly goods. Instead, we should nurture and foster philanthropy as a general principle and virtue to live by.

In the previous chapter we discussed the Stoic view on kindness and the giving and receiving of favours. For Seneca, as the quotation above argues, an act of generosity should not be considered as transactional, and in turn the gratitude from the receiver should not be disproportionate to the favour they have received. One way to avoid the inevitable and thorny questions of benefits given and favours returned is to take money out of the equation. Extremely wealthy people are often described as being 'philanthropists' because they set up charitable foundations. But is this really philanthropy in the true sense? You don't need to be wealthy to be a philanthropist, and it is rather sad that in modern definitions philanthropy has come to be measured by the amount of money billionaires are prepared to give to worthy causes (all tax deductible, no doubt).

The word philanthropy derives from the Greek words *philos* meaning 'love' and *anthropos* meaning 'humanity' – hence a philanthropist is

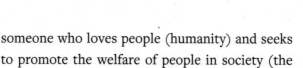

someone who loves people (humanity) and seeks to promote the welfare of people in society (the opposite being a misanthrope). So how can we foster philanthropy in this traditional sense?

Well, we can start by doing simple acts of kindness and consideration such as offering up our seat to an elderly person on a crowded bus or train, or helping them with a heavy burden they may be struggling with. These seem to be very straightforward acts that any reasonable and thoughtful person would do, except stop and think for a moment how often we actually do them in comparison to how often we don't do them – if we are honest with ourselves, more often than not we don't do these things. Another act of kindness could be something as simple as starting a cheerful conversation with a stranger at a bus stop; they may be feeling lonely and isolated and might appreciate the interaction.

In a wider sense we can be philanthropic with our time by volunteering at somewhere like an advice centre, or local foodbank or soup kitchen. Or we could offer our time to teach a particular skill or share some specific expertise that may be of benefit to individuals or groups. The point is to show your love for your community by offering something for nothing. Without monetary gain, the reward is the act itself. As Seneca noted: 'the reward for all the virtues lies in the virtues themselves. For they are not practised with a view to recompense; the wages of a good deed is to have done it'.[115]

---

115   Ibid., Letter 81

8.

IMAGINE THE IDEAL PERSON – IMAGINE THE IDEAL MONSTER

Back in Chapter Three when we discussed the pillars of Stoicism, we looked at a quote from Marcus Aurelius where he mentions the value of recognizing the virtues of people around you, your friends and your family, and making a mental list to 'keep in mind'. We are going to return to this practice now but in an expanded form.

In Letter 45 to his friend Lucilius, Seneca lists what he says makes someone happy. Seneca argues it isn't wealth that makes a person happy but rather their strength of character and the expressions of the virtues that they live by. He writes that a happy person, one who lives with *aretē* and is the best version of themselves, is 'upright and exalted, who spurns inconstancy, who sees no man with whom he wishes to change places, who rates men only at their value as men, who takes Nature for his teacher, conforming to her laws and living as she commands ... who turns evil into good, is unerring in judgment, unshaken, unafraid ... never moved to distraction'.[116]

Let's break down Seneca's list:

A. *'upright and exalted'* = **honest and dignified**

B. *'spurns inconstancy'* = **consistent and faithful**

C. *'no man with whom he wishes to change places'* = **is not envious or resentful**

D. *'takes Nature for his teacher'* = **adheres to the Stoic principle of living in accordance with nature**

---

116   Seneca, *Moral Epistles to Lucilius*, Letter 45 'On Sophistical Argumentation', Wikisource

E. *'turns evil into good'* = **brings good values to bad situations**

F. *'is unerring in judgement'* = **never makes errors of judgement**

G. *'unshaken, unafraid'* = **is bold and courageous**

Wow, that is quite a list of virtues to try to live up to, but that is what this process is about, the process of trying to live as the best version of ourselves. So, and this could be done as a journalling exercise, take a sheet of paper and list people who you admire and why you admire them. Think specifically about their character traits and their virtues, how they treat themselves and how they treat other people. The overall idea is to come up with an ideal human in terms of their virtues and attributes. Think of yourself as a benign Doctor Frankenstein creating the perfect person from the composite parts of your role models and people who you admire. This can also be done in reverse by listing the opposite character traits, ones you abhor. Imagine the worst possible person you can – a monster, but not some horror movie monster, just someone who is self-absorbed, selfish, unfeeling, arrogant, mendacious, etc. Keep the lists somewhere safe (hence in a journal) and review them from time to time, adding new virtues and vices and reminding yourself of that to which you aspire and all that you reject.

9.

RETREAT INTO YOURSELF – GO ON HOLIDAY INSIDE YOUR OWN HEAD

[People] seek retreats for themselves – in the country, by the sea, in the hills ... But all this is quite unphilosophic, when it is open to you, at any time you want, to retreat into yourself. No retreat offers someone more quiet and relaxation than that into his own mind, especially if he can dip into thoughts there which put him at immediate and complete ease.[117]

Meditations – Marcus Aurelius, Book IV

117 Marcus Aurelius, *Meditations*, p23

Throughout his *Meditations*, Marcus Aurelius refers again and again to retreating into ourselves, into the 'inner citadel' of the mind. In a sense the whole of *Meditations* is Marcus undergoing an exploration of how he thinks and feels about life; it is unclear if he ever intended the books to be read by anyone else. Of particular appeal is his suggestion that we can retreat into the calm and quiet of the mind, but it should be noted that this is a meditative practice that takes practise. Think of it as the opposite of the view from above: this time we are not moving outside of ourselves, but moving inside of ourselves, retreating into our mind.

Marcus Aurelius is saying that people seek escape in nature, by the sea or out in the countryside on hills or mountains, but can also escape into the inner peace and calm of the mind. To this end I would suggest the following visualization exercise. Close your eyes and think of a place you have visited that has struck you as representing nature at its most stunningly beautiful and awe-inspiring. I realize not everybody, for any variety of reasons, can be lucky enough to travel and experience some of the world's most spectacular beauty spots, so if this is the case a local park or woodland area can work just as well. Alternatively, choose somewhere, look up pictures on the internet and let your imagination go there. Try to imagine the sounds you would hear: a bubbling brook or waterfall, birdsong or the rustle of wind through the trees. Now try to imagine the smells you might expect: pine needles or freshly cut grass, or the bouquet of wild herbs and flowers. Once you have created this beautiful oasis of calm inside your mind you should feel at ease and free from troubling thoughts and anxieties.

Marcus Aurelius closes this meditation by urging us to remember two important principles: 'First that things cannot touch the mind: they are

external and inert; anxieties can only come from your internal judgement.'[118] In other words, we control what can or cannot enter our minds. And we should realize '... that all these things you see will change almost as you look at them, and then will be no more. Constantly bring to mind all that you yourself have already seen changed. The universe is change: life is judgement.'[119]

As Stoics we must embrace the impermanence of things and remind ourselves of the power of living in the moment, because soon that moment will become the past, and when we recall the past we will see that things have changed.

118   Ibid., p24
119   Ibid., p24

10.

REVIEW THE DAY / JOURNALLING

We started our Stoic day by imagining and anticipating what may befall us in the forthcoming hours. Then we meditated on what lay ahead in preparation for any possible obstacles or issues, and gave thought to how we could deal with anything the day threw at us. Now it's time to review our progress.

Seneca made it a daily practice to review his day. In his essay 'On Anger' (*De Ira*) he describes how he calmed himself at night by his process of reflecting upon the day: 'I pass the whole day in review before myself, and repeat all that I have said and done: I conceal nothing from myself, and omit nothing.'[120] He goes on to write how he thinks about the events of the day and submits

---

120   Seneca, *Minor Dialogues*, pp.76–114

his testimony to himself as if he was speaking in court. Did he, for example, deal with conflicts in an appropriate manner if he feels he 'reprimanded that man with more freedom than you ought, and consequently you have offended him instead of amending his ways'?

Epictetus, too, believed in the value of reviewing the day. In the *Discourses* he describes his step-by-step appraisal of his actions:

Admit not sleep into your tender eyelids till you have reckoned up each deed of the day: How have I erred, what done or left undone? So start, and so review your acts, and then for vile deeds chide yourself, for good be glad.[121]

---

121 Epictetus, *Discourses*, p155

So, go through each event of the day and evaluate and appraise it. Epictetus also suggests we should identify anything we could have done which we didn't and, although 'vile deeds' is perhaps a bit strong, basically be honest with ourselves about any errors we made and how we may make amends.

This is, of course, a lot of thinking to do and a lot of information to assess and appraise, so this is where the practice of journalling comes in. Writing things down helps us to organize our thoughts, separate them from the jumble inside our heads, and see clearly what happened and when, thus enabling us to dispassionately assess them.

There are journalling apps for smartphones and tablets which provide hints and tips and daily challenges to get you into the habit of writing

down your thoughts. But in terms of reviewing your day there is a simple three-step series of questions you can ask yourself which follow the guidelines of Epictetus and Seneca:

A. *Did I attend to and address any faults or bad habits today?*

B. *If I did, was I successful?*

C. *If I wasn't successful, how can I improve tomorrow?*

The practice of mindful and careful daily reflection is a key aspect of Stoic philosophy. For this, we need to build up the resilience to be totally honest with ourselves in identifying our issues and problems. If we are not fully honest, how can we hope to address problems and live as the best version of ourselves? Journalling can be a very useful and powerful aid in this respect and can be finished every night on a positive note with three further appraisals known as 'Good', 'Better' and 'Best'.

Good: What did I do today that was good? Perhaps you did somebody a kindness or a favour, or did some life laundry.

Better: What did I do that I could have done better? (This could be covered in part C above – or could concern something else entirely.)

Best: What was the best that I could have been?

It is very important once you have answered these questions and written them down in your journal that you don't beat yourself up about the negative aspects you have been reflecting on – the very fact you are capable of analyzing and appraising your faults shows you are making progress and taking responsibility. So congratulate yourself on this. It's a sign that you are progressing to where you want to be. Also, on a day when things have gone wrong, always ask yourself if the outcome was in your control. If it wasn't, discard it from your mind and move on. Sleep tight and sweet dreams; tomorrow is a whole new day to practise being a Stoic.

Suggestions for Further Reading

This book has really only scratched the surface; there is a wealth of material to delve in to expand knowledge and understanding of Stoicism, from classic historical texts to modern interpretations and applications.

For anyone wanting to know more about Epictetus' ideas, the *Enchiridion* (usually included in most editions of the *Discourses*) is a good starting point – it was intended as a Stoic handbook or guide. The *Discourses* themselves are denser and require considerable thought and contemplation (be sure to read an edition which is well annotated).

Seneca's essays, such as 'On Anger' and 'On the Shortness of Life', are fun and not only give a good insight into his thoughts, but also show off his prodigious literary gifts: he must have been some orator. For any would-be Stoic, Marcus Aurelius' *Meditations* is an absolute must-read. It is a beautiful book full of wonderful insights, wise advice and melancholy observations.

For modern interpretations of Stoicism, John Sellers' book *Lessons in Stoicism* gives a clear overview on how the ancient philosophy can resonate in the hectic world of today. Ryan Holiday is the founder of the Daily Stoic website and author of bestselling books on Modern Stoicism such as *The Obstacle is The Way* and *Ego Is the Enemy*, which outline how to turn adversity into advantage. Donald J. Robertson is a modern stoic writer and leading authority on Marcus Aurelius, his work draws on practical applications of stoic philosophy and its uses in Cognitive Behavioural Therapy. Robertson's book *How To Think Like a Roman Emperor* applies the writings of Marcus Aurelius to modern mindfulness techniques. Donald Robertson is also the author of a graphic novel/biography about the life of Marcus Aurelius *Verissimus*, which is beautifully illustrated and very readable.

Selected Bibliography

Diogenes Laërtius, *Lives of Eminent Philosophers*, trans. Mensch, Pamela, ed. Miller, James, Oxford University Press, Oxford, 2008

Epictetus, *Discourses and Selected Writings*, trans. and ed. Dobbin, Robert, Penguin Random House, London, 2008

Marcus Aurelius, *Meditations*, trans. Hammond, Martin, Penguin Random House, London, 2006

Nietzsche, Friedrich, *Basic Writings of Nietzsche*, trans. Kaufmann, Walter (1908), Random House, New York, 2001

Sagan, Carl, *Pale Blue Dot: A Vision of the Human Future in Space*, Ballantine Books Inc, New York, 1997

Sellars, John, *Lessons in Stoicism*, Penguin Random House, London, 2020

Seneca, *Consolation to Helvia*, trans. Stewart, Aubrey, The Talking Book, (Kindle Edition), London, 2023

Seneca, *Dialogues and Essays*, trans. Davie, John, Oxford University Press, Oxford, 2008

Seneca, *Letters from a Stoic*, trans. Campbell, Robin, Penguin Random House, London, 2004

Seneca, *Minor Dialogues: Together with the Dialogue 'On Clemency'*, trans. Stewart, Aubrey, George Bell and Sons, London, 1900

Websites

dailystoic.com

modernstoicism.com

wikisource.org

Acknowledgements

I'd like to thank the following people for their help and support in producing this book. Firstly, Nicki Crossley, my commissioning editor at Michael O'Mara Books, for trusting me with the project and for her enthusiasm, patience and support throughout the process, and Louise Dixon for recommending me as someone who may be well suited to Stoicism. Thanks also to my editor Gabriella Nemeth and to Meredith MacArdle, who both painstakingly corrected my sloppy manuscript and knocked it into shape. And special thanks to Rosa Weeks and my family and friends for putting up with some of my less than Stoic responses to things: I am trying to practise what I preach, but it's not always easy – love and hugs to you all.

Index